P.K. PAGE

ESSAYS ON HER WORKS

WRITERS SERIES 6

SERIES EDITORS:

ANTONIO D'ALFONSO AND JOSEPH PIVATO

Canada

Guernica Editions Inc. acknowledges the support of
The Canada Council for the Arts.
Guernica Editions Inc. acknowledges the support of
the Ontario Arts Council.
Guernica Editions Inc. acknowledges the financial support of
the Government of Canada through the Book Publishing
Industry Development Program (BPIDP).

P.K. PAGE

ESSAYS ON HER WORKS

EDITED BY LINDA ROGERS
AND BARBARA COLEBROOK PEACE

GUERNICA
TORONTO·BUFFALO·LANCASTER (U.K.)
2001

Barbara Colebrook Peace and Linda Rogers, Guest Editors
Guernica Editions Inc.
P.O. Box 117, Station P, Toronto (ON), Canada M5S 2S6
2250 Military Road, Tonawanda, N.Y. 14150-6000 U.S.A.
Gazelle, Falcon House, Queen Sq., Lancaster LA1 1RN U.K.

Typeset by Selina.
Printed in Canada.
First edition.

Legal Deposit – Fourth Quarter
National Library of Canada
Library of Congress Catalog Card Number: 2001095257
National Library of Canada Cataloguing in Publication Data
Main entry under title:
P.K. Page : essays on her works
(Writers series ; 6)
Included bibliographical references.
ISBN 1-55071-134-2
1. Page, P.K. (Patricia Kathleen). – Criticism and interpretation.
I. Rogers, Linda. II. Peace, Barbara Colebrook.
III. Series: Writers series (Toronto, Ont.) ; 6.
PS8531.A34Z83 2001   C811'.54   C2001-902453-3
PR9199.3.P3Z83 2001

CONTENTS

ACKNOWLEDGEMENTS

With thanks to Rick Van Krugel, *Canadian Literature, The Malahat Review, Sono Nis Press, The Vancouver Sun, Dundurn Press, University of Toronto Quarterly.* "P.K. Page, The Alchemist" by Linda Rogers, was first published in *The Broad Canvas: Portraits of Women by Women,* Sono Nis Press, 1999.

INTRODUCTION

LINDA ROGERS

A poem, or a life, is as many faceted as a diamond. Its various aspects are known differently, the differences manifested in the many ways a jewel captures the light. This is especially true of the gemologist, P.K. Page, who has revealed so many facets of her truth that it can only be known in the quiet, unrefractive space behind the eye of the beholder. The various contributors to this collection of "fabules" about the enigmatic poet and painter all experience her canon uniquely. As she has played with the light; sometimes the painter of occult landscapes, sometimes the flashing gypsy dancer, sometimes the impatient gardener in Paradise, Page is to each an exotic storyteller.

The poet Dylan Thomas described the one story all writers are channelling as the dialectic progression of birth copulation and death. For Page, the story is cosmic. Her details are brushstrokes in an impressionist painting, always in movement, usually the gyre that takes us in and out of empirical reality, its ultimate truth in the circular movement of existence. Like Virginia Woolf, Page is a fabulist, her conversations baroque, at once knowable and unknowable as the mysteries find their only resolution in moments of revelation. For those who need to pin down the moment, as each question leads to another larger question, the experience is dizzying.

In Travis Lane's essay, we sense the frustration of the one child in the front row at a magic show who must know how the magician performs his tricks, something Page, like all magicians, who have a code to protect their secrets, will not do. If she is indeed the alchemist, "transmuting lead and bread into gold" as Atwood tells us in her poem, then she has the right to assert the alchemist's prerogative and remain invisible in the poems.

Page once told me her one wish as a lifelong life observer has been that she could make herself small as Alice in order to go unperceived through the keyholes of those hidden rooms where mysteries reveal themselves in glorious transformations only the small are privileged to witness undetected. Every contributor to this book agrees on one thing; that, written large or small, Page is an exquisitely sensible medium for something special passing by, shadows surrounded by light, gilded by her ecstatic appreciations.

It has been difficult for a woman who has the formidable beauty of Greek sculpture and a legendary voice to go unnoticed, to abandon the "I" when she would be the "eye" in the poem. She will not be pinned down. She will not explain the tricks that reveal the mysteries she would have us experience so that we are changed as she has been in what Susan Musgrave describes as "pure poetry" blessed with the absence of ego.

Lois Crawley's photo-essay about P.K. in 1946 is a silent movie, an observation of the observer in which there is no dialogue. This essay captures the grace which is essential to magic. Not exactly spells, Page has assured us that her work is play. Even though she seems to be juggling moons and stars in her many ceremonial moments, there is always a sense of delight in the process of high seriousness. She is at once the magician and the child suspending her disbelief in the possibility of transformation. This playfulness is captured in Carole Matthews' description of a friendship defined in cryptic language and an endearing totem, Mr. Koko, also separate, intransigent and uncapturable as P.K. or the metaphorical duck Brian Bartlett discusses in his essay "For Sure the Kittiwake," which first appeared in the journal Canadian Literature.

The confabulist loves the tools of her trade, the stream of words that is a river of stars flowing through the knowable universe, but words are only anthills and mountains, aspects from which the river is seen. Ultimately, they are songs without words. Atwood, who is also perceived as a cool priestess of language, explodes as her ironic and appreciative poem about the "Non-Snow Angel" heats up to a "splendid burning" we cannot own but only observe as it "breaks the mundane horizon."

In their essay, Lucy Bashford and Jay Ruzesky pin down the poet uncomfortable with stasis as she is frozen in her own arras, a film of one of her stories. It is an interesting moment revealing the compulsion to move in the physical and spiritual journey that has no end, as the incandescent pearl keeps circling like the silver bracelet on her wrist, which she twists in a characteristic gesture captured by Crawley, coating itself in more layers of light.

Every poet has a favourite poem. P.K. says hers is probably "Arras," where the enigmatic peacock in his erotic unfurlings displays the unspoken energy of creation. Poet Patricia Young, herself sensible to the ruin and beauty in a fallen world, assures us that is all you know and all you need to know about P.K. Page. She and Harold Rhenisch give us classroom insights that reveal her passion and frustration with the material world.

In the following critical essays and more personal recollections of fellow writers, P.K. is known and unknown in various ways. My co-editor Barbara Colebrook Peace, who with Kelly Parsons has fashioned a collaborative discussion of praise and shadow in the conversational tone of this collection, shares my wish that you will also delight in the jewelled surfaces of this dialogue between Canadian writers and critics, all of whom have been generous with their time and trouble.

One poet could not contribute. Because he was at the end of his life and no longer had the strength to write, Al Purdy wished me to express his great admiration for P.K. and the wish that he could have done more. Now he is with the angels and, in truth, may always have been, as is P.K. When Niki Goldschmidt "Mister Opera Canada" commissioned *The Invisible*

Reality, a millennial oratorio in eight movements based on her poetry, it was decided the Archangels should come in, "as they always do," in D major. Nothing less than a major key for this major poet "smoothing the holy surfaces."

P.K. PAGE AS A NON-SNOW ANGEL

With Apologies to "The Snowman"

MARGARET ATWOOD

Mystical, practical P.K. has rolled round,
at least her birthday has. Look, here is one
surprised O topping another, and

to complete it, an open-mouthed or whistling zero.
Not 80! No,
impossible! Say, rather, ageless.

Wingless, as well, although it's more
as if she's got
wings, than has not.

But wings of what?
Of paper, or of words, or of pure air,
which all our words are

made from: and of wordless
amaze, as well. Thus winged and wingless,
see how she soars

above the earthy earth! But that's
inaccurate; for though she flies,
it's through the earth, rather
than beyond it. If an angel, one

that's dug a garden and worn hats,
and numbered

the bulbed and knobbly inventory
of the body.
Though her inner eye

may well unfurl
itself, and see the world
on fire, an incandescent pearl,

that splendid burning's earned. Therefore, our dear
sublunar alchemist and paradox, who has
transmuted daily lead and bread to gold

for us, may you preserve
in your seraphic and ferocious garden, where
the flowers are fanged and tentacled,

the vivid animals reverse
their naming and revert to essence,
and a new sun

of unknown
and elegant colour
breaks the mundane horizon.

P.K. PAGE, THE ALCHEMIST

LINDA ROGERS

I am a tin whistle
Blow through me
Blow through me
And make my tin
Gold

If ever a swan was born in Swanage, it must be Patricia Kathleen, eldest and only daughter of Lionel and Rose, sister to the mythically beautiful Michael, who in his infant photographs could be the future Siegfried, so perfect is the strength and beauty of his face. The family mouth and curls, the stature, must have set brother and sister apart from other children the moment they both sailed out in their pram.

The public P.K. is a woman described in the words of fairytale. She is handsome, a goddess, commanding, majestic, the Aurora for her time, dressed in swansdown or, more likely, something sculptured from a store that sells wearable art. Her jewelry could be borrowed from the border of a medieval illumination.

My husband calls P.K. The Jeweller. Her beautifully crafted poems are, from every angle, the literary equivalent of the Imperial eggs the artist Fabergé created for the Royal Family of Russia, precious jewels articulating the surface of a holy idea.

Dazzled by the dramatic readings that have made Page the Dowager Queen of Canadian poetry, we have become familiar with one aspect of a complex intelligence. She is bright. Her poetry is brilliant. The brilliance, which finds its resonance in all the references to light and precious metal, reflection, in her poetry is insight. For some, even her grand-daughter, Christine, who uses the word in her loving essay "My Grandmother's Luggage," it is "intimidating."

P.K., who has made a study of philosophy and Sufism, may be willing the sea to lie down as she would iron the wrinkles on the surface of the earth in one of her most beautiful poems. There is underpainting she would calm with her meditations and "holy surfaces." In medieval painting, a ground of red bole gives the gold leaf its vibrancy. Only the blood surging beneath the stories of snow disturbs the serenity of Page's art.

Images, P.K. believes, are out there in the phenomenal world, like pears on a tree, for artists to select. In spite of the apparent craftsmanship of her work, she says that, unlike writers who stick to schedules, she is undisciplined in the regularity of her devotions, that the lines summon her to the writing desk. The discipline came in the beginning when, as a teenager, she made herself write a sonnet a day, all of them, she says, bad. It was practise and much reading that made the ink flow smoothly.

The daughter of an army officer, P. K. inherited

the stature of that fine horseman who joined the
cavalry because it provided the opportunity to ride
for a living. Not "the very model of a modern Major-
General," he taught her that joy is the fundamental
premise of work. Her father also possessed a sense of
humour, the playfulness that marks his daughter's
obsession with line and language.

Her social composure aside, there is turbulence in
the inside air of the poems that resonates on the
surface, giving them a dynamic that pulls the reader
in. P.K. says she was always an outsider, the stranger
who watches and listens. She has an eye for detail and
a good ear. A tall girl with a funny accent who did not
attend Sunday School, she felt "different" from the
beginning. This may have been the impetus for the
antithetical moments in her personal journey, which
sometimes led to conflict.

There are a number of poems about conflict and
resolution, which have, even in this time of unbridled
revelation, an astonishing candour. What child hasn't
craved "forgiveness for thy just rebukes as I still crave
thy praise?" Startled by the "thys" of this poem, I once
asked P.K. if the Bible had been her primer. Despite
the fact that the poet did time in an Anglican school,
her parents were religious non-conformists, which partially explains her attraction to eastern philosophy.

In the gravity defying air-filled skirt of the whirling sufi is found her personal archetype, the circle (or
eye, "I") that dominates both her writing and the
painting which came later in life when the voice
detoured in colour and silence, the visual poetry of

her middle-age. Painting, which surprised P.K., as C.S. Lewis was surprised by Joy, is the gift of her mother, Rose, daughter of an artistic family, who illustrated the poems P.K.'s father sent home from the front for their infant daughter. She is perhaps the gypsy P.K. sometimes allows us to glimpse in herself. It is the gypsy who calls her work "play," which all art might be and all artists, in the vernacular of The New Age, still their "inner children." As P.K. says in "Traveller, Conjuror, Journeyman":

> Play, perhaps. Not as opposed to work. But spontaneous involvement which is its own reward; done for the sheer joy of doing it; for the discovery, invention, sensuous pleasure. "Taking a line for a walk," manipulating sounds, rhythms.

There are stories of P.K. as a young woman at the time Canadian poetry was in its adolescence, when poets became a tribe. P.K. danced on tables, I have heard. She threw back her head and laughed. But, there were factions, even then. Her initiation to the politics of poetry came with the *Preview* Poets, writers like Patrick Anderson and F.R Scott, themselves scholarly and intimidating, who took the young poet into their cell. In grand opposition, stood that baroque individualist Irving Layton, who suggested a literary purgative for the likes of those he saw as the embodiment of Wasp repression.

The outspoken and sometimes careless Dorothy Livesay was another angel to wrestle. They had disagreed about poetry, about style, but P.K. wrote the now famous poem around a promise Dee had made about "rhyming in heaven" which says Amen to that. In that poem, she says "magnets pull us together and we go for each other." It is an interesting and revealing line about someone preoccupied with the properties of metal. Freud said conflict is the mother of creativity. When you read through the canon of P.K. Page and search the paintings for clues to the character of the eye that has seen and recorded so many human events, you begin to know the daughter of sun and moon in terms of alchemy, gold and silver.

She refers to her fictitious gypsy and real progenitors as if they were armies inside a walled garden, one in the house and one camping in caravans. They are the figurative seat of the negative attraction. P.K. Page may well be the Queen of Canadian poetry, but the gypsy lurks. You catch the flash of her silver jewelry, the flirtatious locus of her moving skirts.

P.K. kept the English love of garden and language and an accent that stops at about the place the Titanic sank. Perhaps her desire to embroider comes from an obsessive reaction to dust and endless horizons. She is still English, in the enclosed garden where poets like Edith Sitwell and fellow émigré Anne Szumigalski flourished.

When P.K. married the widowed Commissioner of the National Film Board in Ottawa, where she had been working, she assumed the life of a corporate wife. Arthur Irwin, a recent centenarian, was a management bureaucrat and diplomat, who worked with my uncle, Dana Wilgress, Canadian Ambassador to London, Moscow and Nato, in External Affairs, another cross-reference in this family fabric. Diplomatic missions in Brazil, Australia and Mexico with her new husband awakened the painter and shushed the poet who found her pen looping and cross-hatching, hungering to put down the shapes of her new landscapes, and, eventually, when courage filled her diplomatic elbow length gloves with paint, the colours as well.

P.K. does tell one story about letting the gypsy out in her diplomatic life. She was having lunch at Government House with the Queen Mother and her various aides. P.K., who probably knew you never ask the Queen Mum (who, at home, apparently refers to herself as an "old Queen" in her household of elderly male servants) a personal question did ask a personal question. The Queen Mother, astonishingly, talked about fatigue making one vulnerable, whereupon P.K. asked if she had ever been invulnerable. It sounds perfectly logical, but the Queen Mum waved her sceptre and P.K. was "levitated" and left on the cold side of the room. She had accomplished invisibility.

In the Major key, Page has written fine public poetry like the beautiful glosa "Planet Earth":

> It has to be made bright, the skin of this planet
> till it shines in the sun like gold leaf.
> Archangels then will attend to its metals
> and polish the rods of its rain.

These are words she would like us to remember.

The gypsy has sometimes shown her face boldly in poems and paintings about private life. These are the domestic sketches which have their literary equivalent in poems like "Deaf Mute in a Pear Tree," where his "locked throat finds a little door and through it feathered joy flies screaming like a jay."

P.K. was always a painter, even before she knew it. Poets are required to capture truth in snapshots, or in the case of such a colourful writer, in paint and precious metal so that the eye becomes the "I" of the poem and we see with her clarity.

We know from her writing that the moon has a dark side. Like all of us, she has had her disappointments. There has never been a child of her own making to crown with the glory of gold sunlight in her tempera paintings. The angel she wrestles now is very real. It lives in her, in the bones that ache and torment her.

As one grief piles on another, an exhausted world, the death of friends, the act of God that brought down a favourite Douglas fir tree, she continues to be, in accordance with Mother Theresa's direction to all of us, "a pencil in the hand of God." This is the confidence instilled by parents who also taught her a responsibility to her gifts and the will of a woman determined to iron the wrinkles and gild the ceremonial moments.

One night when she was small, P.K.'s mother took her outside; indicating the night sky she asked, "How can we believe in only one way when heaven is so various?" These are the landscapes behind the eye which accommodate every possible variation. The sky may have been the permanent home to an army child who moved so often her mother refused to make jam because she would have to pack it around.

She could still be watching for those messengers she writes about who bring truths from places more evolved than Planet Earth. P.K. says if she were a dictator she would command that everyone read Doris Lessing's "inner-space fiction," *Shikasta,* which puts forward the premise that there is intelligence greater than our own and made Page believe she was "hearing the truth for the first time." There are voices out there. They dictate the poems which she "sometimes understands later." Between the poet and the voices there are arras curtains of her own making, on which she transcribes her worlds and ours.

A READING OF P.K. PAGE'S "ARRAS"

PATRICIA YOUNG

ARRAS

Consider a new habit-classical,
and trees espaliered on the wall like candelabra.
How still upon that lawn our sandalled feet.

But a peacock rattling his rattan tail and screaming
has found a point of entry. Through whose eye
did it insinuate in furled disguise
to shake its jewels and silks upon that grass?

The peaches hang like lanterns. No one joins
those figures on the arras.
                    Who am I
or who am I become that walking here
I am observer, other, Gemini,
starred for a green garden of cinema?

I ask, what did they deal me in this pack?
The cards, all suits, are royal when I look.
My fingers slipping on a monarch's face
twitch and grow slack.
I want a hand to clutch, a heart to crack.

No one is moving now, the stillness is
infinite. If I should make a break . . .
take to my springy heels . . . ? But nothing moves.
The spinning world is stuck upon its poles,

the stillness points a bone at me. I fear
the future on this arras.
                              I confess:
It was my eye.

Voluptuous it came.
Its head the ferrule and its lovely tail
folded so sweetly; it was strangely slim
to fit the retina. And then it shook
and was a peacock – living patina,
eye-bright, maculate!
Does no one care?

I thought their hands might hold me if I spoke.
I dreamed the bite of fingers in my flesh,
their poke smashed by an image, but they stand
as if within a treacle, motionless,
folding slow eyes on nothing.
                              While they stare
another line has trolled the encircling air,
another bird assumes its furled disguise.

P.K. Page wrote "Arras" in the early 1950s, sitting in
an Australian garden under a magnolia tree, the fra-
grant smells of which were so compelling she had to
wrench herself out of her chair in order to go inside
and find a dictionary. She tells me that in the course
of working on the poem she had written "maculate,"
and wanted to check its multiple meanings. When she
read in the dictionary that "maculate" could mean
"dark spot" as well as "region of greatest visual acuity
in the retina" she was delighted. In the context of her
poem, the word suggested both the messy wildness of

the creative force as well the importance of the eye as portal to the mind and soul. Although P.K. will not say that "Arras" represents her (for how can a single poem represent any poet?) she does say that "Arras" is one of the poems she is most pleased to have written. Not surprisingly, this poem presents a complex landscape upon which P.K. explores her ongoing fascination with human perception and its role in the creative process.

From the outset there is a marvellous swiftness to "Arras." In just a few lines the poem moves from the "trees espaliered on the wall like candelabra" to the narrator (who, in this poem, I think it is safe to say, is P.K. herself) standing on the lawn in "sandalled feet." No sooner have we been introduced to the "arras" when out of nowhere a peacock enters the scene, "rattling his rattan tail and screaming." In an instant, the still green world is changed, shattered, "smashed."

Like everything on the arras, "the peacock" is motionless, "folded," until it passes through the narrator's retina. That is, until the eye receives the peacock, and the imagination transforms it, the image of the bird lacks depth. Having passed through the poet's eye, however, the peacock throws off its "disguise" and reveals its true identity, an identity which both startles and demands attention. When the bird "shake[s] its jewels and silk upon [the] grass," it is not only expressing its peacock nature, it is also disturbing the two-dimensional world of appearances; it is disrupting conventional, linear thought. This, then, is true sight: to see beyond the single, literal peacock to the essence of peacock, peacock as life force. As one would expect, this life-embodying peacock unleashes a kind of chaotic energy upon the tranquil arras, transporting the narrator, vaulting her up and over – unexpectedly and despite herself – into another state of consciousness.

Though there are a number of oblique references to others in this garden, the poem is strangely devoid of human beings. We read of body parts rather than whole people. The poem speaks of "our sandalled feet," "their hands," and their "slow eyes." An over-whelming sense of physical restraint also pervades the garden. The narrator's fingers "slip" and "twitch," while the others in the garden simply "stand" and "stare." To the narrator, this beautiful but static garden is claustrophobic, unbearable, and all the more reason to welcome the peacock's unbridled feathery display. Where, the poet seems to ask, is the relief in a world of infinite stillness?

As a teacher of poetry P.K. has often spoken of the need for the poet to get out of her own poem and let the words and images speak for themselves. In class and in conversations she has argued against the intrusive "I," the ego-driven "I," the "I" that keeps standing up in front of the movie screen and blocking the audience's view. How then to understand her insistent use of the word "I" in "Arras," particularly in stanza three? And yet, how not to write "I" when exploring the subject of individual perception? How not to use the word when writing about the "eye,"

that astonishing organ through which the world enters the consciousness? P.K.'s repeated use of the
pronoun "I" is, of course, intentional and serves to
echo and mimic the noun, "eye," itself employed four
times in the poem. And "eye[s]" are everywhere in
this poem. Some are "bright," and some are dull and
"slow." Most notable are the many "eye[s]" on the
peacock's "lovely tail," those extraordinary markings
which contribute to the bird's aura of almost mystical
vision. Throughout "Arras," P.K.'s recurring use of
"I" subtly draws attention to the literal "eye," thereby
reinforcing its central role in the poem. After all, one's
"eye" must be wide open in order for the transformative peacock "to insinuate" itself.

As mentioned, the others in the garden are
sketched in so lightly they are almost immaterial; they
remain detached, unmoved by the peacock's flamboy-
ant exhibition. This is understandable when one realizes that the peacock, or any image for that matter,
is in "disguise" until it finds "a point of entry." In
contrast, the narrator is enthralled by the "peacock-
living patina, / eye-bright, maculate!" and tries to
convey what she sees to those around her. Until she
attempts to communicate her experience she feels a
kind of self-imposed guilt as seen by the "bone" which
"points" accusingly at her. She wonders, though, how
others will react if she were to "make a break" or
disrupt their well-ordered conception of reality. "Do
I dare disturb the universe?" she seems to be asking.
The fact that the narrator would like to "take to . . .
springy heels" after, and not before, receiving the

image into her eye, perhaps also indicates that she now feels, like the peacock, a new found sense of recklessness.

After some deliberation, the narrator answers the question she herself posed earlier in the second stanza; she "confess[es]" that it is her "eye" through which the peacock found "a point of entry."The use of the word "confess" here suggests an element of doubt, even a reluctance to admit it was her "eye." This hesitation perhaps arises out of the narrator's fear that others will not understand, or, what is worse, not care to understand. She embraces the image of "the head" and "lovely tail" reluctantly because she knows there is a price to pay. The narrator may "want a hand to clutch, a heart to crack" but in this garden she is surrounded, overwhelmed even, by indifference. Perhaps, too, the narrator momentarily resists confessing what she has seen because she realizes it is futile to attempt to verbalize an essentially private experience; she also understands that human perception is as varied as it is untranslatable.

Having told us why she admitted entrance to the peacock – because it was "Voluptuous" and "its tail was folded so sweetly" – the narrator expresses disappointment. The "hands" she hoped would hold her if she "spoke," and the "fingers" she "dreamed" might "bite" her "flesh" do not touch her. There is no human contact, no engagement or mutual understanding. It is as though the others in the garden are not equipped with even the basic physiological apparatus necessary for literal sight: their eyelids "fold . . ."

not over "a point of entry" but over "nothing." Such eyes are frighteningly blank, without pupil, iris or retina, and denote figurative blindness. Is it any wonder, then, that the narrator "fear[s] / the future on this arras."

Although temporarily transported to another level of consciousness, the narrator is still aware of how she must appear on the "arras," that "green garden of cinema." She is both "observer" and "other." As such, she is able to view herself objectively while existing within a subjective state of mind. The twin sign of the zodiac, "Gemini," also suggests a split or dual nature. The narrator is torn between the desire for love and companionship and the need to exclude others in order to concentrate on her private visions, and the creation of her art. She also realizes that once she has admitted the peacock into her eye, she has alienated herself, become incomprehensible to others. This, in turn, frightens her. She feels herself losing control: "My fingers slipping on a monarch's face / twitch and grow slack." These lines create a dream-like sensation of reeling backwards through space, and thus the plea for "a hand to clutch, a heart to crack" can be seen either as a cry for someone to enter into the multi-dimensional world within her consciousness, or as a cry for someone to pull her back onto the arras where predictable patterns of thought predominate.

Like the "arras" itself, the "cards" dealt to the poet are one-dimensional, flat. We are also told "all suits, are royal when [she] look[s]," again suggesting the structured, formal world of appearances. Are we to infer then that the tapestry is peopled with rigid, vacuous aristocrats whose very presence contributes toward the poet's sense of suffocation? Or do these "cards" with "monarch's faces" appear in the poem in the same way images appear in dreams – out of nowhere, making their own kind of sense? Have these face "cards" risen up out of the poet's unconscious, and do they therefore defy categorization or explanation? Perhaps it does not matter that we know who or what these "monarchs" do or do not represent. More important is that we feel the narrator's desperation, her need to "break" from the world associated with these kings and queens and jacks. More important is that we feel the narrator's desire for "a hand to clutch, a heart to crack." On a visceral level we feel her longing for connection with someone, anyone, who not only sees what she sees but who also exists in the flesh and blood, three-dimensional world.

In "Arras," heightened perception leads to creativity and creativity is inextricably linked to sexuality. As mentioned, the narrator is seduced by the peacock's irresistible beauty almost against her will. Once the peacock enters her mind, she experiences an orgasmic sense of release; finally she is free of the inhibiting restraints of linear perception. The peacock is the source of her delight and as such is phallic shaped: "Its head the ferrule and its lovely tail / folded. . . sweetly." So tenderly do these words express the narrator's feelings toward the peacock that they could be words spoken by a lover to describe

her beloved. Just as the penis fits perfectly into another "point of entry," the peacock "fit[s]" the retina.
By alluding to the sexual act, P.K. reinforces the deep
and perfect union between poet and image. The use
of the peacock as a sexual image is also particularly
appropriate in this context because, of course, it is
during the mating dance that the male bird spreads its
tail and screams. One can almost imagine P.K. throwing up her hands and admitting she has no justifica-
tion or rationale for succumbing to the peacock's
allure other than it is beautiful – "living patina /
eye-bright, maculate."

Though the language and imagery of "Arras" are
grounded and concrete there is an elusive quality to
the poem. Just when the reader thinks she understands the poem's intention in a particular line or
stanza, that understanding seems almost to slip out of
reach. When I ask P.K. what "Arras" means she
responds by saying "a poem should not mean, but be."
And then she adds, "The poem is a labyrinth of the
self," which is the sort of answer I should have
expected of a poet who has written a poem riddled
with phrases such as: "through whose eye...," "who
am I...," who am I become...," "It was my eye."
Fascinating too is the fact that P.K. admits that the
poem remains mysterious even to her. Though she
wisely resists trying to explain the poem, P.K.'s few
comments help confirm what I, as a reader, have come
to suspect: that the poet had as little control over the
actual writing of her poem as the narrator of "Arras"
had over the peacock's entrance into her eye. How

appropriate, then, that at the end of the poem we are left with the evocative and open-ended image of P.K. sitting in an Australian garden years ago, pen in hand, receptive, alert, "eye-bright," waiting for "another line" of poetry to write itself.

While recognizing the difficulty, if not the absurdity, of attempting to pin down such an enigmatic poem, I will venture to say that for me "Arras" is about the necessity of "smash[ing]" the "poke" inside of which we all mentally exist; it is about the "Brain-break . . . ," the "Mind-break . . ." P.K. speaks of in another short poem entitled "Concentration." Only by breaking through our restrictive perceptive boundaries can we free the artist within. Or, in P.K.'s words, only when we figuratively "break the bones of [the] head," and "the fontanelles open / a fraction of a second" can "something shimmering whiz . . . out." Among other things, "Arras" is also about shifting and altered states of awareness. It is about the sexual nature of creativity as well as about the solitary pleasures experienced within the mind. Redolent with images of light and dreams and beauty, "Arras" is, at one and the same time, about the inherent loneliness of human consciousness as well as the "Voluptuous" visions exploding behind "the retina."

P.K. IN THE CLASSROOM

PATRICIA YOUNG

It is 1977 and Derk Wynand has asked P.K. Page if she would like to teach a poetry workshop in the Creative Writing Department at the University of Victoria. Derk sweetens the deal by offering P.K. what he believes will be his best class that term, a second year poetry workshop. Reluctantly P.K. agrees. I am registered to take this class. I am also eight months pregnant.

Before the first class I go to P.K.'s office to introduce myself and explain that I will have to miss some of the workshops once the baby is born. P.K. invites me to sit down and we talk. About what I don't remember – poetry, babies? – but I like her immediately. She is warm and gracious and somehow in these few minutes she makes me feel special and good about the imminent birth of my daughter.

In class P.K. introduces us to poets she has loved for years – Yeats, Stevens, Rilke. Especially Rilke. She brings copies of their poems to class, passes them out and reads them aloud. She does not ask that we analyze these poems; she just asks that we listen. Though we are young and unpublished, P.K. assumes we are writers and will continue on this path. To this end, she insists we keep a journal because, as she says, a journal is a well from which we will learn to draw. And she gives weekly assignments, asks us to write poems using syllable count, half rhyme, hidden rhyme, assonance, dissonance, alliteration. I haven't yet read P.K.'s poem, "Remembering George Johnston Reading," but if I had I would know she is offering us the poet's tools, those chisels and hammers and files that will help us create "the poem's skeleton and ornamentation."

P.K. does not critique or edit our poems. In this way, she is different from the other Creative Writing instructors we have had and will have in future. In her beautiful voice, with its slight English accent, she speaks the words of great poets and we are mesmerized. What is more, she treats our poems with the same respect as she treats the poems of her favourite poets. She treats the very notion of poetry with a kind of reverence.

At the end of term we submit our journals, which P.K. will not grade, and our revised poetry manuscripts which she will. When P.K. returns my manuscript I read her comments over and over. Among other things, she says that my poems are fuzzy, unfocused, not sure of what they are trying to say. Later, at my mother's house I collect Clea, my daughter, along with diapers, toys and bassinet. Before leaving I show my mother P.K.'s remarks.

"Och, well then," my mother says, "you'll have to listen to P.K. You'll have to write more clearly."

I smile at this irony. Like many daughters, I am hesitant about writing anything, clear or otherwise, because of my mother. Surprisingly, her response also makes me feel a sense of relief. It is as though she is giving me permission. Permission to what? To go elsewhere for guidance, a sense of connection? Is this the moment I begin to move away from my mother whom I love and who wishes me well but who has no interest in poetry or the artistic imagination?

On a conscious level, it does not occur to me that P.K. represents the possibility of a spiritual or artistic mother. I have not considered the concept nor do I know of any such relationships. But I do feel myself drawn to this poet and teacher; I feel myself drawn to her wisdom and visionary way of looking at the world. And the attendant glimmerings of guilt? Of course. I feel them too for they are the result of any severing.

Many years later at a party, Derk Wynand, another of my early poetry instructors, mentions, casually, that P.K. refused to teach in the Creative Writing Department after her experience that year.

"What experience?" I ask.

"What year?"

"You know," says Derk, "the year she taught you and Gail and Mark Jarman and all those others."

"What others?" I say, baffled.

"Oh," says Derk, "I think Harold Rhenisch was also in that class, and Neile Graham."

Derk tells me P.K. was so disheartened by the closed-mindedness of the students in that second year workshop that despite Derk's entreaties, she refused to go back into a classroom. She said she could not bear the thought of more students who had already decided they had nothing to learn.

My mouth falls open. "No," I say, "impossible. We were never that bad."

And then it comes back to me. How we balked at P.K.'s suggestions to experiment with other forms, to read other poets, to try writing poems that were not "I" centered. It comes back to me: how we feared being influenced. How we insisted on complete freedom, on being able to write what we felt.

It comes back to me: our overriding concern with the purity of our own voices. I remember a slightly exasperated P.K. saying to my friend Gail Harris and me that our general lack of attention was going to be the death of us some day.

Derk has wandered off.

I multiply my own youthful arrogance by twelve or fifteen, and am chastened.

In the days following this revelatory conversation with Derk, I think about those long ago workshops, all of us with our heads in the clouds, the mud, or at least in some other place, and I ask myself what, if anything, did I take away from them. So many hours. The rain beating down or the sun shining through the huge seminar room windows. I ask myself the question every Creative Writing instructor and student asks him or herself at some time or other: can poetry be taught? I decide it can and it can't. I decide that if Derk, the rigorous editor, taught me no word, line, or stanza is so sacred it cannot be tossed out, then P.K., the metaphysical thinker, taught me, just by her example and presence, that the writing of poetry is a sacred calling.

It is 1978, a lovely day in April. All over campus blossoms float from the trees. My bicycle leans against the Clearihue building and, as usual, I am leaking milk. I run up the stairs to P.K.'s office to say goodbye and wish her a good summer. Perhaps I understand she has affected me deeply but, if asked, I could not say how. I am awash in the confusion of my own life and have no idea that over the years P.K. will become my friend, my confidante, my single most important role model.

SEEING WITH THE EYES OF THE HEART

Praise, Shadow and Dimensions
of Eternity in the Poetry of P.K. Page

BARBARA COLEBROOK PEACE

AND KELLY PARSONS

> *One eye sees, the other feels.*
> Paul Klee

I

PRAISE

> *Distilled from all this living,*
> *all this gold.*

P.K. Page is a metaphysician in the best sense of the word, and deserves to be named among the twentieth century's great visionary poets. It's the work of a visionary poet to see deeply into the heart of things. Arising from this seeing, the next and most natural step is to praise. Praise has been a part of poetry from ancient times; so much so, that poets in ancient Greece were called "praise-singers." Rilke thought that praise was the essence of a poet's task: "Oh, tell us, poet, what you do? – I praise" (*Spate Gedichte* 160, 1921). Modern poets have increased the range of subjects for praise, opening for example to Pablo Neruda's praise of socks, or Page's praise of a new bicycle, "aglow in the furnace room / turquoise where turquoise / has never before been seen." For Page, the entire universe is interconnected, and that is why a bicycle can be as transformative a vision as daffodils were for Wordsworth: "Lightly resting on the incised / rubber of its airy tires / it has changed us all."

Page's writing has a quality of luminous interiority reminiscent of certain medieval women mystics, such as Mechtild of Magdeburg and Hildegard of Bingen, whose praise poetry honours the earth. With incantatory power and profound impact, in the poem "Planet Earth," for example, Page wakes us to our intimate connection to the earth and everything on it, and to the responsibility inherent in this bond. It is nothing less than the collective heart of humanity that must, before it's too late, reach out its hands and "newly in love, / we must draw it and paint it / our pencils and brushes and loving caresses / smoothing the holy surfaces." We must all fall in love with "this great beloved world and all the creatures in it," perhaps for the first time. In the glosa form, Page takes inspiration from four brilliant lines from Neruda, lines that in lesser hands would be near impossible to live up to. Images of the skin of the planet and the earth's surfaces as lovely big textiles represent qualities to be touched, appreciated and cared for with reverence, as Page begins to expand upon in her first four lines of the glosa:

> It has to be loved the way a laundress loves her
>   linens,
> the way she moves her hands caressing the fine
>   muslins
> knowing their warp and woof,
> like a lover coaxing, or a mother praising.

The poem is astonishing in its achievement of rhythm, rhyme, assonance and alliteration. It is quite simply a tour de force. We must all open our eyes – see with one, feel with the other – as Page calls us to a spiritual ecology:

> The trees must be washed, and the grasses and
>   mosses.
> They have to be polished as if made of green brass.
> The rivers and little streams with their hidden
>   cresses
> and pale-coloured pebbles
> and their fool's gold
> must be washed and starched or shined into
>   brightness.

Hers is a poetry that serves the planet, that serves life. What Pages sees beneath the apparency of things is gold. In waking us up to the world, she praises it, and in praising she goldens it. We find in her work the "gold smiles" of angels, the "golden rain of poems," and "heart the sun." Page serves the natural world by seeing it deeply and praising what she sees. Sometimes her work is breathtakingly beautiful; it seems to aspire to, and indeed achieves, the same purpose as manuscript illumination in the Middle Ages: to draw attention to, to embellish, to glorify. In a section of the long poem "Melanie's Nite-Book," look at how the poet praises:

> The world gold-leafed and burnished:
> gilded trees,
> leaves like a jeweller's handwork,
> grasses, ferns
> filigreed and enamelled – Byzantine.
> Cresses in clusters, bunched
> beside a stream –
> a glittering gold chain,
> gold mesh, gold sheen,
> where I bent down to drink.
> (What bird then sang?)
> Gold water in my mouth,
> gold of my dreams
> slipping like sovereigns
> through my gold-rinsed hands.

Here is a fine and beautiful example of Page "gold-ening" the world. Everything touched by her inner eye is gold, is elevated, or spiritualized. This is the work of her praising eye, her alchemical eye. This is perhaps her mystical third eye at work, which is the twinning of her seeing and feeling eyes.

The poem "Three Gold Fish" is also about this kind of seeing; the fish "burned and shone / and left their brand – / a piscine fleur-de-lys / stamped on the air, on me, / on skin and hair / spinning to giddy heaven."

One immediately thinks of the Sufi dervishes, and their whirling prayer-dancing. Page often uses the word "giddy" to describe heightened spiritual states: "You . . . / walked giddy with gold / your gilded name grew in our heads and shone." When we're giddy we're on the verge, brimming, filled; a brush loaded with paint is a giddy brush. Page herself is exactly this kind of loaded brush.

Page has apparently served an apprenticeship with the "Flowers of the Upper Air . . . in timeless Time at their green leafy school." In an exquisitely euphoric gesture of reverence, she writes: "Oh, tree! I say as I whiz past, bowing. I bow. I whiz / powered by some high-octane fumeless fuel / that spring has invented. Oh, tree! Tree. Tree!" The poet sees a world where "the sun is sharpening every leaf. / Its threads are spinning a golden tent."

Alchemist of the heart that she is, she has learned here – and passes it on to her readers – that while the body greys the heart goldens.

Page wonders about the world, about the human heart: "Who would think that this old hive / housed such honey? / Could one guess blue and gold of a macaw / blue and gold of sky and sun / could set up such melodic din / beat so musical a drum? / Distilled from all this living, all this gold." She tells us that "some there are, fearless, touching . . . the wonderful soil, nameless, beneath their feet." This is such tender and simple praising, this is "loving the thing for its thingness." In a similar spirit, the spirit of being deeply available to the present moment, poet and Zen master Thich Nhat Hanh has said that the miracle is not to walk on water, the miracle is to walk on earth.

Page offers us an example of experiencing joy by choice, and encourages us, rather than suffering, to "choose instead / meadows flower-starred / or taste, for instance – just for an instance – bread. / The sweet-smelling fields of the earth / dancing / goldenly dancing / in your mouth."

II

SHADOW

O Shadow, take my hand.

From ancient times, praise-singing is often accompanied by a shadow, the sense of loss of that which is praised. Pindar, in the middle of an Olympian ode praising human achievement, breaks off to ask "What is Man?" and answers "a dream of a shadow." So too in the Psalms, praise and lamentation go hand in hand. More recently, Rilke refers to Lamentation as the sister of Praise in Sonnet VIII: "Only in place of Praise, Lamentation . . . "

For Page, seeing with the eyes of the heart means seeing the whole, the shadow with the golden. In her key poem "After Rain," she asks that "pears upon the bough" may "hang golden in / a heart that knows tears are a part of love." Throughout her work, the beatific vision of the golden is balanced by images of grief, loss, the denaturing of the earth, the vanishing of colour and warmth. These shadow poems are often etched in black and white; snow is a recurring image. "Such blacknesses abound / I know not in or out. / O Shadow, take my hand" ("Dark Kingdom").

The shadow of loss may be long, stretching deeply into the past, as it does in Page's poem "T-Bar" ("the old wound aches again," referring to the Edenic myth of ancient separation between male and female) or far into the future, as in her apocalyptic prose work "Unless the Eye Catch Fire." Whether in the past or future, Page often presents loss in terms of the colours, the golden, going out of the world. In "Unless the Eye Catch Fire," colours take on an extra significance, and the ability to perceive "the colours" becomes symbolic of transcendence in a dying earth. At the end of "They Might Have Been Zebras," the seven forlorn monosyllables of the final line fall on our ears like a bell tolling: "Is this grey ash all that's left?"

A poem equally of praise and lamentation, "They Might Have Been Zebras" moves between shadow and sunlight, through black and white to golden to grey. Encountering four raccoons in the early morning, the poet notices how different it is to see them out of their usual night-time context, "utterly foreign to morning's minted light." Often in Page's work, something is stripped of familiarity to be seen completely fresh, newly created: "And I see them blacker and whiter than I had dreamed / sharper, more feral . . . " This is seeing with the eyes of the heart; it is also seeing them in the aspect of eternity, as they really are. We are drawn into the poem to see them with her eyes: ". . . by day they immobilize me. I hold my breath. / Turn to a great soft statue with inflammable eyes / tinder for the fire they strike from the morning air." Now we can see the lines we quoted earlier in this essay more clearly in their shadow context, and notice that it's only after the poet's eye catches fire that she perceives the goldening of the world: "The sun is sharpening every leaf. / Its threads are spinning a golden tent." The poem's ending leaves us with a sharp sense of loss: "But the four who blinded me are gone." We feel, like the narrator, bereft, as she awakens us – "Is this grey ash all that's left?" – to a premonition of loss, of precious creatures vanishing from our world.

"Leviathan in a Pool," another "black and white" poem, is a lament for captive whales. The opening image shocks us: "Black and white plastic / inflatable / a child's giant toy." This is the whale, desecrated by commercialisation. The theme of desecration of nature is taken up in "T-Bar," where black and white are the only colours, the white of snow, the black of machinery, the black and white of bride and groom. The poem's emphatic first word, "Relentless," resonates throughout the whole, speaking of the movement of time, and of the way we spread ourselves and our machinery over the wild, primaeval landscape ". . . the empty T-bars keep / in mute descent, slow monstrous jigging time." But though in a sense we impose time on the landscape, humans are also seen here as "wards of eternity." In one of the brilliant metaphysical re-envisionings of the world for which Page is famous, she sees the cable car occupants "pass through successive arches, bride and groom, / as through successive naves, are newly wed / participants in some recurring dream." Here is an image of classical perfection, the perfect symmetry of pairs, polar opposites, black and white, bride and groom, a symmetry echoed in the formal design of six line stanzas, each with their alternating sets of direct or slant rhyme. It makes a formal music extremely pleasing to the ear, like a Bach cantata. Yet under that beauty, we hear an organ sound dissonant chords. Words of pain are the ground notes of the poem, swelling in adjectives, nouns and verbs: "Relentless, monstrous, broken, haemophilic, uncertain, lost, spastic; automatons, incision, pain, wound, rubber band; aches, jerked, snaps, catapults." The clocks "peck" as well as sing – extraordinary and marvellous choice of verb! This is a poem about the impossibility within a time-bound world of perfect human love, and the powerlessness humans may experience in a denatured world of their own making. The poem moves in a ritual dance, a fearful symmetry, between beauty and pain, time and eternity, machinery and nature, love and separation. This moving, beautiful and complex shadow poem is another example of Page seeing with the eyes of the heart.

Snow in Page's work is not always seen as purely beautiful. Just as in "T-Bar" she refers to snow as "haemophilic," so in another shadow poem, "The Snowman," she startles us by calling the thaw "leprous." The more startling, because this follows right after the image of a child building a snowman.

Perhaps it's because we are so used to seeing snow, lulled by the crooning of Bing Crosby, that we need this jolt. This is Page's dramatic ability to see the

shadow of something we have always taken for
granted as conventionally beautiful. The second part
of the poem presents a chilling nightmare vision: "But
once I saw a mute in every yard / come like a plague;
a stock-still multitude / and all stone-buttoned, bun-
faced and absurd." Again, colour goes out of the
world, as it did after the eternal vision of raccoons,
so we are left with grey: "and greyed a little too,
grown sinister / and disreputable in their sooty fur
/ . . . in a landscape without love."

Page's "black and white" poems include several
others with imagery of snow; two outstanding ones
are "Photos of a Salt Mine" and "Stories of Snow."
Since these are mentioned in other essays in this book,
we will leave them to the reader to explore, turning
finally to one of Page's most beautiful poems, "Elegy." In this poem the word "black" occurs three
times, along with "blackness," and "black-edged,"
"darkness" (twice), "night," and "nightshade." In
contrast to this we have "white" (twice) and "whiteness" and a glorious "golden" section in which the
past is praised and remembered. Again, we see how
lines quoted in the first section of this essay deepen
when read in their shadow context: "You, white and
sewn with scarlet once, / walked giddy with gold /
your gilded name grew in our heads and shone." It is
their very pastness – the word "once" tolling in our
ear – that gives these images their power to lacerate.
Though the "you" addressed in the poem seems a
beloved person, we could also read this supremely
beautiful and moving poem as an elegy for the earth:

And if we cry now it is because your green tree
turned most rapidly into coal
and because we have seen our whole hearts
and known them black-edged as mourning
    envelopes.

We emerge from the shadow poems with an appreciation that Page does not turn away from suffering, grief and loss; she has a "heart that knows tears are a part of love." When we return to the "golden" visions we see them shine the more brightly for the surrounding dark.

III

DIMENSIONS OF ETERNITY

*Where now a new
direction opens like an eye.*

In Page's prose poem "The Arrangement," tall presences from another reality set the narrator a task, a puzzle: to arrange eight "celestial sticks." "'Make of them a form,' they said, 'recognizable, complete and unconfining. The one condition: that the sticks all point the same way.'" The narrator spends years making forms, the same forms over and over: "A fence, a line, bannisters, a wall." She is aware, however, of being locked in by these dimensions and seeks another way: "But what other way? What other direction? What other form? I knew no other. North, south, east, west. Up, down, right, left. What more?"

That cry of frustration, "What more?" articulates a problem that confronts every artist, poet, or indeed human being.

Similarly, in her essay, "Traveller, Conjuror, Journeyman," Page expresses her desire for "a world larger than the one I normally inhabit," and comments: "At times I seem to be attempting to copy exactly something which exists in a dimension where worldly senses are inadequate. As if a thing only felt had to be extracted from invisibility and transposed into a seen thing, a heard thing." Many of Page's poems are a kind of dialogue, an exchange between "this habitation – bones and flesh and skin / where I reside" ("Dwelling Place") and that "timeless Time," the dimension "where worldly senses are inadequate." She always has her eye to "that tiny chink where two worlds meet." In that chink, the self is seen as being simultaneously here on earth and in eternity: "It has a leafy smell // of being young in all the halls of heaven." This dual aspect of the self is essential to her poetry. The task, the problem confronting any artist interested in eternity, is how to render the one in terms of the other.

Page's exquisite poem "The Maze" affords an excellent example of how she achieves this. It begins very naturally, with the poet talking to herself about a memory: "I clearly recall the feel of the clipped hedges – / laurel or box – I am not sure which. / I was still small / so the little leaves of box / would have seemed bigger." The tone is quite low key and matter-of-fact, and the image of the maze is real and earthy, right down to the detail of whether the hedge was laurel or box. She continues to give us sensual details that render the maze's, and her own, physical reality: "I remember they shone, looked black in places, scratched / the skin of my wrists and ankles as I passed." That is the end of the first stanza, and so far we are still very much here on earth. At the beginning of the second stanza, however, we sense a change in the key and tonality of the music:

> Overhead the sky was light,
> a faint cirrus,
> duck-egg changing to golden like a wing,
> but the shadow cast by the hedge
> threw a chill upon me
> as I kept to the curve that drew me in
> and in.

Though still on earth, the poem opens now to the sense of sky, and the lyrical "duck-egg changing to golden like a wing" introduces an image of flight, and goldenness, moving us towards the dimension of eternity. Interesting that in this poem, we are given both the golden and the shadow, "the shadow cast by the hedge" following right after the golden. The next lines take us much further out:

> Compelled, and carrying out a strange instruction –
> vital, timeless, tangible as a thread –
> I was tracing the spiral nebula in my head.

Page has taken us on a journey with her, still rooted

in physicality, and the transition to another dimension is effected so gently that, as in a dream, we are now somewhere else and it seems natural that we should be. For we are now in "timeless Time." We begin to realise that this is a cosmological journey, and also a journey within the self, or as the Sufis would say, a "journey to God in God." The poem's transcendent ending speaks of a desire:

> hoping to pass that place on the sharpening turn –
> to grow small, then smaller, then smaller still – and enter
> the maze's vanishing point, a spark, extinguished.

This is the death of the self, "a spark, extinguished." Not physical death but what Rumi and other Sufis have spoken of as "fana" or "self-annihilation," death of the false self, the ego-driven life, so that one can have union with the divine and eternal. Page wants to "un-me myself" as she says elsewhere. In "The Maze," Page succeeds brilliantly in rendering the infinite in terms of the finite – for what could be more finite than a maze?

Two other poems, "A Backwards Journey" and "Chinese Boxes," also speak of things that grow "small, then smaller, then smaller still" as far as infinity. The idea of a shape being enclosed in another shape exactly the same is known as "self-symmetry," and it's clearly something that fascinates Page, for it occurs often in her drawings as well as in her poetry. It's witty and typical of a metaphysical poet to choose something not ordinarily considered poetical. "A Backwards Journey" focuses on that very mundane object, the Dutch Cleanser can the narrator remembers from childhood. The poetic lines fit inside each other in a lovely echoing of their subject: "around which ran / the very busy Dutch Cleanser woman / her face hidden behind a bonnet / holding a yellow Dutch Cleanser can / on which a smaller Dutch Cleanser woman / was holding a smaller Dutch Cleanser can . . . "Page, fascinated by this phenomenon as a child, already had a sense of infinity and its power: "And at that moment / I think I knew that if no one called / and nothing broke the delicate jet / of my attention, that tiny image / could smash the atom of space and time." It's interesting that in both "The Maze" and "A Backwards Journey" we have the self remembering the self as a child. There is a sense here that we ourselves contain infinite selves – growing smaller and smaller, or larger and larger, depending on the point of view.

"The Maze," "Chinese Boxes," and "A Backwards Journey" are all poems of solitude, the self talking to the self. But Page has also written several poems in which she encounters visitors or messengers from another dimension, who bring blessing and comfort. Always in these poems, the narrator moves through to a new recognition. The task facing a poet who wishes to speak of such messengers, without being stymied by conventional imagery of angels, is even more daunting. How does she do it?

In "Invisible Presences Fill the Air" the narrator

senses the unseen presences first as great birds "I hear
the clap of their folding wings." That sound is somehow convincing, in a way that a visual description of
their wings could not have been. Later, she senses
them as horses "I feel them breathing on my cheek. /
They are great horses dreaming of flight." Because she
appeals to auditory and tactile senses rather than the
visual, Page does manage to convey a physical reality
with which we feel engaged. Something else about
these messengers is equally convincing: that the narrator feels them first as birds and then as horses
"dreaming of flight"; they are, of course, both and
neither, and this very fact is typical of the dreamlike
state. As in "They Might Have Been Zebras," and
"Unless The Eye Catch Fire," these presences are
associated with fire and they affect a transformation
of the narrator's heart. "When in my heart their
hooves strike flint / a fire rages through my blood."
Similarly, in "The Yellow People in Metamorphosis"
the narrator experiences the presences with her auditory and tactile senses: "Stamp. Stamp. I feel them
weighty / Wonderful acrobats clanking about / loud
in the next dimension."

In "Presences," a remarkable glosa, Page again
evokes beings from another place and time: "Extraordinary presences, the sunlight seeming / to light them
from within." "And when they turned to us, their
brightness spilled / over our skin and hair, and like a
blessing, there they were as our guests, accepted and
accepting." Again, there is a movement from shadow
to golden, "led us from the shadows to the sparkle /

of Aten-light." It is characteristic that "only our golden selves went forth to meet them." Golden is the self seen in the aspect of eternity.

One of the most beautiful and moving of the "visitant" poems is the glosa "The End," which tells of a beloved who returns from death to speak with the narrator: "And one, composed of light, came back . . . " He comes to tell her something of what death is like, and the other side of death. Though it remains a mystery, "nor can I possibly tell you," yet he comforts her, "When your turn comes you'll know." This poem too is transformative, for after the vision, the narrator understands "it was clear to me now there was nothing to fear / and no reason for anyone, here or anywhere / to suppose he will be drowned / when he's held by the sea's roar, motionless, there at the end." The poem ends in a recognition of the essential unity of human beings: "For he belongs to the sea – we all do. We are part of its swell."

"Another Space" also speaks of presences from another dimension, who "in a circle on the sand / are dark against its gold / turn like a wheel / revolving in a horizontal plane / whose axis – do I dream it? / vertical / invisible / immeasurably tall / rotates a starry spool." These presences draw the narrator: "Down the whole length of golden beach I come." The presences are seen, though perhaps not completely: "I see them there in three dimensions yet / their height implies another space . . . " and this leads her to "speculate / on some dimension I can barely guess." The presences of this poem do not just remain a vision; they change the narrator deeply, "And something in me melts. / It is as if a glass partition melts – / or something I had always thought was glass / some pane that halved my heart / is proved, in its melting, ice." This poem speaks of transformation, "where now a new / direction opens like an eye."

It is this transformation that allows Page to find "a world larger than the one I normally inhabit." Indeed, in her poems we encounter vast spaces and the dimensions of eternity. This is rare in lyric poetry – for a parallel, one would have to go to epic poetry, Homer, Virgil, Dante and Milton – or perhaps to Eliot or Rilke, poets with whom Page has much affinity.

At the end of the prose poem "The Arrangement," quoted at the beginning of this section, the narrator finds at last the puzzle's answer, the transcendent form that answers the cry of the human heart, "What more?" "The simple starry form and the spokes pointing one way in. To the centre. Spokes of a wheel!" We, her readers, are extremely fortunate that Page has found the way in, to the centre. Fortunate that her poetic forms are indeed "recognizable, complete and unconfining."

Above all, we are fortunate that she has succeeded so brilliantly in her task, to extract "a thing only felt" from invisibility, and transpose this into "a seen thing, a heard thing."

Page is a poet who can take something as ordinary, small and overlooked as a Dutch Cleanser can, and make us see it in the perspective of infinity. She can make us hear the clank and feel the weight, almost touch the "Wonderful acrobats clanking about / loud in the next dimension." Praise, shadow, and dimensions of eternity are so interwoven in her work that we return from reading her poetry with the sense of a much larger world than the one we normally inhabit. A shadow world within a golden world; a golden world within a shadow world. Page gives us hope for this planet and hope for the self, world within world, in which we live against the stellar background of the cosmos. The words she once wrote of the embodied self, "It has a leafy smell / of being young in all the halls of heaven," might aptly be spoken of her poetry, for it is both of the earth and of eternity.

UP AGAINST THE WALL

Or, Learning to Live Without a Map

HAROLD RHENISCH

When presented with an impenetrable wall, there are many possible approaches, short of retreat in the fog: you can scale the wall with crampons and ropes, ever mindful of boiling oil; you can paint over the wall, then walk into the painting; you can adjust your imagination so that the wall is no longer there. P.K. Page taught me how to do the latter. Her teaching career spanned a few months in the early winter of 1978 in a second year Creative Writing workshop at the University of Victoria. The impact of two of her incidental statements from that time changed my life.

P.K. put me in my place. At that time when I was first beginning to consider that to become a poet might not be a promethean presumption, I would force myself to sleep no more than six hours a night in order to have the time to read. And read I did, about thirty pounds of books a night – enough to stuff a queen-sized pillow case to bursting. I was not selective, but tried to read everything, and at breakneck speed, too: Schopenhauer, Nietzsche, Wordsworth, Pound, Hemingway, Beowulf, Bergson, Euripides, Rilke, Kant, Rimbaud, and a thousand others, fifty versions of *Snow White,* and whole shelves full of

musty anthropological journals that made me sneeze
as I read between the scurrying book lice. I added each
book like a butterfly pinned and mounted in a glass
case. It was an honest attempt at international travel,
but it had a crippling flaw: I understood hardly a word
I read. I was barely conscious after all. During that
time I wrote a very mythic poem in which the trout
in a stream became trout, stream, and poem all at the
same time. I had written myself into a mental country
I did not recognize. I wanted a map. I was surrounded
by bush.

"What is reality?" I asked my instructor, the poet
Derk Wynand, that day.

Poor man. About all he could do to that question
was raise his eyebrows and look troubled. "I'm serious," I said. "I know," he answered. "But I don't
know what it is." Then he added in what tried to be
a reassuring voice, "Keep looking." I recognize that
country pretty well now, but there still aren't any
maps. I know now that they would just get in the way,
but back then, by the time the February rains hit town
the whole attempt at absorbing world literature and
philosophy left me feeling like I was standing at the
bottom of a seamless stone wall three hundred metres
high and vanishing into fog. That rock wouldn't
budge and there was no way to get over it. That's
where P.K. stepped in. I was writing sprawling mythic
poems, bright in imagery and for the most part totally
incomprehensible. "Harold," she said. "You have to
understand: no poet ever wrote a poem by working
hard, but by being incredibly lazy. Poets sit around

doing nothing for a long, long time. They are very
irresponsible. Then a poem might come." I left town
for a week, went to the mountains, and went fishing.
The poems came.

P.K. showed me what my place was. In the midst
of all my dread seriousness she introduced me to the
poems of Lorca and Rosenblatt, bright, sunny, and
musical, all painted in clear, bold colours in direct
sunlight. It has become a kind of oracular cliché that
no-one can teach anyone else to write and that the
most that young writers can hope for is a benevolent
mentorship, yet it's not mentorship that P.K. gave me.
She gave me a glimpse of wisdom that only revealed
itself to me years later. Trying to define wisdom
would be like trying to define reality (oh no), yet
P.K.'s words do, I believe, spring from it: "Anyone
who can write a poem," she said, "can also paint a
picture. The two arts come from the same source."
To me at that time, with only a rudimentary sense of
form, music, and imagery, this contention seemed not
only foreign but peculiar as well. I took it as a
statement of personal philosophy, applicable to P.K.'s
gifts, but inapplicable to my own. Well, two decades
have come and gone. Whenever I find myself caught
by the temptations of philosophies and grand systems,
lose my path in their gridworks and find myself
standing below that massive granite wall or in a
blinding, plutonium sunlight as the sun reflects
equally off every droplet of fog, I remember P.K. If
laziness doesn't get me out of there, then drawing
does. For someone caught up with words to a rather

extreme degree, to give words all up and intuitively follow the same designs through the world without latitudes and longitudes of words is a delicious and healing luxury. It is like coming home. It is like sweeping the light clear of obstructions.

P.K. has not been my only guide in literature, of course, yet in all my years in the Interior of British Columbia, a little removed from literary society and often glimpsing it only out of the corner of my eye as it goes by the orchards and forests with trumpets and red velvet capes, with psaltery music and jugglers throwing oranges, and leather-gloved women carrying proud, fierce hawks on their wrists, along with the faith of a few distant poets, the company of artists and the imagery, inquisitiveness, and inclusiveness of visual art have sustained me.

FOR SURE THE KITTIWAKE

Naming, Nature, and P. K. Page

BRIAN BARTLETT

Who am I, then, that language can so change me? ...
Where could wordlessness lead?
                    Page, "Questions and Images"

                    ... the whole business of naming is curious.
                    Page, *Brazilian Journal*

I

Can poets take too much pleasure in words? How much should our language frustrate and shame us? How much excite, tickle, and teach? Is taxonomy the hand of death, murdering to dissect? Do you feel that your own name – Patricia, Arthur, Eve, Adam – pigeonholes you? "Why should three phrases alter the colour of the sky. . . ?" (Page, "After Reading Albino Pheasants"). Is a name a cage, a crown, a straitjacket, a coat, a shell, a nail, a halo, a brand, a bridge, a prison cell, a pointer, a window, a cross?

2

In P. K. Page's early poetry, children and adolescents are often rambunctious. Look at those in "Young Girls" – porpoise-like, giggling, lolloping, very prone to smiling and crying. In contrast, the title figure of "Only Child" seems quiet, solitary, overshadowed by his mother, torn between his need for her and his desire for escape. This poem – one of Page's most full-fledged, suggestive narratives – begins:

> The early conflict made him pale
> and when he woke from those long weeping
> slumbers she was there
> and the air about him – hers and his –
> sometimes a comfort to him, like a quilt, but more
> often than not a fear.
>
> There were times he went away – he knew not
>   where –
> over the fields or scuffing to the shore;
> suffering her eagerness on his return
> for news of him – where had be been, what done?
> He hardly knew, nor did he wish to know
> or think about it vocally or share
> his private world with her.
>
> Then they would plan another walk, a long
> adventure in the country, for her sake –
> in search of birds. Perhaps they'd find the blue
> heron today, for sure the kittiwake . . .

In other poems Page sees girls thrilling to "a phrase / that leaps like a smaller fish from a sea of words" or talking "as if each word had just been born – / a butterfly, and soft from its cocoon" ("Young Girls," "Sisters"). The boy in "Only Child," rejecting his mother's example, has little taste for words and language, as becomes still clearer later in the poem. He seems to resent questions and discussions; he even prefers not to "think . . . vocally." Many of us can sympathize with his reluctance to speak, recalling childhood times when our backs stiffened to parental questioning, even of a kind-hearted, undemanding sort. We can sense false pretences behind the supposed family bonding of the walk (surely "they would plan" is ironic, the mother laying down the plan, and "for her sake" hinting who gained the most from the jaunts). Yet in the poem's second stanza the boy can frustrate us just as he frustrates his mother. For the moment, we might get a grasp on her position, as the boy's evasiveness deprives us of a clear idea of his walks alone. Not only is he evasive with her; he seems oddly out of touch with his own experience ("He knew not where," "He hardly knew, nor did he wish to know"). It's as if he wants a world too "private" for words, or for self-knowledge of any sort.

3

For weeks, "Only Child" has been running river-like – sometimes subterranean, sometimes bursting into the surface – through my other reading. To chart that river, I'm also surveying the surrounding landscape, which is crisscrossed with various writings by Page and by many others. A personal history of reading a poem can include reading reminiscences prompted by the poem, unexpected detours and digressions, through a region of thickly interconnected moments like the jungle lines in one of P. K. Irwin's more intricate paintings.

4

In a *Writer and Nature* course I just finished teaching for the first time, I was struck again by how often our species in its Western variants has been suspicious of its urges to name and categorise. While in European cultures and their descendent cultures in North America there have been innumerable "nature as book" metaphors, nature has also been defined as beyond or outside language. Take a look at Dickinson's poem 811. In other poems Dickinson is perfectly adept at finding riddles, scriptures, and languages in the woods and fields, but in 811 "we" systematize what nature does spontaneously and unwittingly: "We conjugate [Nature's] skill / While she creates and federates / Without a syllable."

Taxonomy is a special villain of the conjugation. Some writers have agonized over its cramping, shrinking effects. In *The Tree,* John Fowles – once a natural-history curator in Dorset as well as a novelist – tells of visiting the eighteenth-century garden of Linnaeus, who did more than anyone else to solidify botanical taxonomy. While Fowles doesn't deny that Linnaeus shaped an extremely useful tool for science, he admits he finds "nothing less strange, and more poetically just, than that he should have gone mad at the end of his life." For Fowles, taxonomy aggravates our tendency to being "a sharply isolating creature," overemphasizes "clearly defined boundaries, unique identities," and "acts mentally as the equivalent of the camera view-finder. Already it destroys or curtails certain possibilities of seeing, apprehending and experiencing."

For all its perceptive moments, there's lots to argue about here and elsewhere in Fowles's book. For instance, didn't Linnaeus help create cultural features through which visceral, emotional, and poetic responses to nature – not just rigorously scientific ones – could arise? Can't the use of a camera encourage and enhance certain ways of seeing? Would Fowles complain that reading one poem keeps us for the meantime from reading another, or that taking one walk keeps us from taking another? From one angle, can't Linnaeus be seen as a non-isolationist, one who wanted not to focus on a few select species but to see and appreciate flora in all its mind-bewildering-and-charming variety?

5

It's no secret that acts of naming and categorizing have been considered more male than female, hooked in with male desires to exploit and dominate. That may be a cliché with all too much historical truth behind it. But in "Only Child" Page reverses the stereotypical difference. The boy is the one who hates labels, the one apparently attracted to sympathetic experience and identification, while the mother is the pointing taxonomist, the person keen with words. The gap between mother and son grows increasingly clear in the poem's middle stanzas:

Birds were familiar to him now, he knew
them by their feathers and a shyness like his own
soft in the silence.
Of the ducks she said, "Observe,
the canvas-back's a diver," and her words
stuccoed the slaty water of the lake.

He had no wish to separate them in groups
or learn the Latin,
or, waking early to their song remark, "The thrush,"
or say at evening when the air is streaked
with certain swerving flying,
"Ah, the swifts."

Birds were his element like air and not
her words for them – making them statues
setting them apart,
nor were they facts and details like a book.
When she said, "Look!"
he let his eyeballs harden
and when the two came and nested in his garden
he felt their softness, gentle, near his heart.

She gave him pictures which he avoided, showed
strange species flat against a foreign land.
Rather would he lie in the grass, the deep grass of
    the island
close to the gulls' nests knowing
these things he loved and needed near his hand,
untouched and hardly seen but deeply understood.
Or sail among them through a wet wind feeling
their wings within his blood . . .

On a first, too-hasty reading, I figured Page was
creating an easily disliked cardboard figure of a

mother to help us empathize with the lonely, sensitive
boy. Soon I started to wonder if a more complex
mother hid behind the son's caricature, and to see that
Page hardly presents the boy's bond with nature as a
perfectly healthy contrast to his mother's. What the
mother is, beyond her protectiveness, curiosity, and
memory for bird names, we can't say; by and large
the poem is much closer to the boy's point of view.
Yet the poem sees him critically as well as sympatheti-
cally. Of what is his relationship to nature made? Not
much. He returns from his solitary walks as if blank-
minded. Just as he has no interest in names, books or
pictures, he apparently doesn't have much in observing behaviour either. He's so absorbed in his personal
experience that images of distant species mean nothing to him. Would the "strange" and the "foreign"
leave a more curious, imaginative boy so cold? It's as
if this boy won't imagine nature beyond his own small
sphere, as if to him "nature" doesn't exist beyond
what he can see with his own eyes and hear with his
own ears.

For the young character in Page's poem seeing and
hearing don't seem nearly as important as feeling.
What does he feel? Mostly, a strong sense of self-identification with the birds –"a shyness like his own / soft
in their silence," "his element like the air," "their
softness, gentle, near his heart." I'll leave to others
the psychological implications of nature as mother
substitute, surrogate nest or womb, haven from
harsher realities. Rather than exploring, the boy
seems content just lying passively in deep grass. His

view of nature is a narrowed one indeed, even sentimental – little like that of Heaney's boy figure in "Death of a Naturalist." Even the gulls seem uncharacteristically silent, especially for gulls around their nests. (One morning a few years ago I stepped cautiously among dozens of egg-pillowing gull nests and had my ears filled with outraged cries, with the warning, feathery shudder of swooping bodies.) Where are brambles cutting arms, flies biting legs, rain chilling feet, owls swallowing mice?

Halfway through the poem, it seems clear that the boy is interested less in the birds per se than in arousing certain sensations within himself, a feeling of "their wings within his blood." Self-identification reaches its peak, and some kind of "setting them apart" might not be such a bad idea after all. Among the trickiest lines in the poem are: "these things he loved and needed near his hand, / untouched and hardly seen but deeply understood." What is it to deeply understand what's hardly seen? Does the boy love the birds he would not name, or is he more in love with his own feelings of being blissfully one with it all?

6

The boy's fondness for the gentle, the soft, and the passive connects to a kind of dreaminess questioned by other Page poems. Sometimes in her work, peacefulness, rest, and inactivity are needed before a release into a dream world of truth and revelation. Other times, they're signs of lethargy, directionlessness, or timidity. The lost, wandering anti-hero of "Cullen" becomes "content to rest within his personal shade" and – in lines very reminiscent of "Only Child" – "felt the gulls / trace the tributaries of his heart . . . " Before his uncommitted and desperate volunteering when war breaks out in 1939, Cullen's weakness of character is laid bare: "Nor could his hammock bear him for it hung / limp from a single nail . . . " The dangers of "gentleness" take an extreme form in "Stories of Snow": "gentle" snow tempts lost woodsmen to "dream their way to death."

It would be going too far to say that the boy of "Only Child" is drawn to a death-like state. But compared to, say, the title figure of "Blowing Boy" – who is very active, kite-like, and associated with language ("In the liquid dark / all his words are released and new words find him") – this boy seems withdrawn, almost listless. Did he ever grow tired of lying dreamily in the deep grass, ever leap into the water to swim and feel surges of energy far from his misty identification with gentle birds and his suspicion of naming?

7

Contrast the boy's indifference to phrases like "The thrush," "Ah, the swifts," "Observe, the canvas-back" with Page's own naming of birds in other poems:

– red-eyed vireos ("Short Spring Poem for the Short-Sighted");

– a hoopoe "weightless upon my wrist, / trembling brilliant there" ("At Sea");

– mallards "unmoving as wood"; and a ruby-throated hummingbird, "a glowing coal / with the noise of a jet" ("Domestic Poem for a Summer Afternoon");

– finches that "stir such feelings up – / such yearnings for weightlessness, for hollowing bones, / rapider heartbeat, east / west eyes" ("Finches Feeding").

And contrast the boy's apparent lack of close observation with all the uses of binoculars in Page's poems (and in *Brazilian Journal*). Page's satirical poem on travel, "Round Trip," mentions binoculars in a traveller's luggage, but the man in the poem is too caught up in fantasies, fears, and foolish dreams to ever use them. In "Visitants," pigeons' brashness and beauties are appreciated through binoculars. In other poems, magnifying devices even become compatible with inner worlds: a scene is examined by "the valvular heart's / field glasses" ("Personal Landscape"), "My telephoto lens makes visible / time future and time past" (the glosa "Inebriate"), and there is a "dream through binoculars / seen sharp and clear" ("Cry Ararat!"). The last poem says "the bird / has vanished so often / before the sharp lens / could deliver it," which expresses skepticism about the device in the face of elusiveness. However, imperfect as they are, binoculars appear too often in Page's work to be merely invasive tools of the devil; they can be useful

without being clinical, they can inspire attentiveness
without aggression.

8

It seemed under a smile of good fortune and good
timing that last week just after finishing Page's *Brazilian Journal* I saw Canadian jazz flautist and soprano-
sax player Jane Bunnett perform with her friends
from Brazil and Cuba. For three hours, with untram-
melled energy and layered sound-textures, the six
musicians evoked Brazilian colours and rhythms as
Page did in her prose of 1957-59. When Bunnett first
heard Celso Machado imitate bird and animal sounds
with his assorted whistles and tiny percussion instru-
ments, maybe she felt something like Page did when
she was first surrounded by the calls of Brazilian birds.

The *Journal* rings and echoes with inquisitive,
witty, sometimes almost ecstatic, observations of
natural scenes. At times Page doesn't know the names
of things but describes them with voluptuous, vivid
detail. A "finchlike bird of a clear cerulean blue with
a black eye-mask and throat" was "so neatly feathered
he looked carved and polished from some mysterious
blue stone, his wife dull green and blue." A bird "like
a ballerina – tiny, black, dressed in a white tutu – flew
out onto mid-stage, did a fabulous *tour en l'air,* and
disappeared before I could further observe it." Of
course, not knowing the name of something can
prompt an observer to describe it more precisely than
otherwise. But it wouldn't be fair to say that Page's
ignorance of the names determines her precise de-

scriptions. Knowing names for animals hardly keeps her from describing them with close attention. A toucan is seen "with an electric blue eye, a bill like an idealized banana, a body of sculpted soot set off by a white onyx collar and gorgeous red drawers," and shrimps are unforgettably seen "with their wide-ranging antennae, looking half like a caricature of a guardsman, half like a nervous pianist, their anxious white front legs like fingers uncertainly playing the same music over and over." (And what of this description of homo sapiens? The curator of a natural-history museum has "dog's eyes – pale eyes, honey-coloured – and I thought, 'Nonsense, look at his nose,' and his nose too was a dog's. And so I switched to his teeth – pointed, white, dog's teeth. Uncanny. But such a polite dog. Wouldn't cock his leg just anywhere.")

One day after visiting a museum Page admits a dislike of stuffed birds, and another day she feels sad at the sight of thirty-some bird-whistles used by hunters to attract birds. ("Are there really so many birds worth shooting?") Yet nowhere in the *Journal* does she suggest that names themselves are traps, cages, luring-to-death whistles, or that – in the terminology of "Only Child" – they turn birds into statues. Early on she even complains about having only "inadequate bird books," and a year later she's still saying "I'd give a great deal for a good bird book." At times her delight in names is obvious. She discovers that birds she'd known in Australia as bellbirds are called ferreiros (blacksmiths) in Brazil, "with good reason. Their song is exactly like the ring of metal." She learns that a variant of the mangrove cuckoo is known in Portuguese as *alma de gato,* "soul of a cat."

Contrast the boy of "Only Child" and his attraction to birds possessing "a shyness like his own / soft in the silence" with Page of the *Brazilian Journal* and her fascination with another kind of bird: "we saw a small, blue-back bird apparently jumping for joy. He was sitting on a fence-post and on the count of five up he went, about a foot in the air, singing. He was not catching anything, as far as we could tell, nor was he showing off for a mate. He was just jumping for joy on a fence-post in the middle of Brazil – for longer than we had the patience to watch . . . In all my amateur birding, I have never seen anything like it." No instant reference to her heart or self, no preference for the gentle and the comforting. Just astonishment at a bird's buoyant energy, at its apparent pleasure and humour. When Page came to write her series of prose meditations "Traveller, Conjuror, Journeyman," she described her own sense of art in terms that echo the Brazilian bird's hopping: "Play, perhaps . . . spontaneous involvement which is its own reward: done for the sheer joy of doing it; for the discovery, invention, sensuous pleasure. 'Taking a line for a walk,' manipulating sounds, rhythms."

9

"Only Child" is here in the background, like the theme forever present in an improviser's mind. It's song and message and object, but also catalyst, spur, hub, home plate, mind seed.

10

Go farther afield for contrasts: Thomas, the adolescent hero of Czeslaw Milosz's novel *The Issa Valley:*

> . . . the Latin names appealing to him because of their sonority: Emberiza citrinella for yellow-hammer, Turdus pilaris for fieldlare, Garrulus glandarius for jay, and so on. Some of the names were conspicuous for their proliferation of letters, forcing the eyes to jump continuously from his notebook to the antiquated ornithology at his elbow. Even the longer names, if repeated often enough, acquired a pleasant lift, one of them, that of the common nutcracker, being absolutely magical: Nucifraga caryocatactes.

This expresses a love of language itself as nourishing, sensuous like the tang of cooked rhubarb, blackberries bursting in the mouth. I think of Page's lines "the word / quick with the sap and the bud and the moving bird" ("Virgin"). Nevertheless, Milosz shows that a fondness for names isn't a simple matter. Young Thomas cares so intensely about his knowledge of nature that when his Aunt Helen uses his bird book as a substitute for a missing bedpost foot he's exasperated by her ignorance. In that scene, Milosz has enough ironic distance to suggest a streak of pride in Thomas's hugging of his knowledge.

Despite qualms and questions about hunting,

Thomas values guns and shoots at birds. We hardly
have to read the several passages about the thrill of
hunting to realize that his approach to nature isn't
simply reverential. Naming itself, for all it's celebrated, is also suspect: The notebook proved that
Thomas had the gift of concentrating on things that
excited him.

> To name a bird, to cage it in letters, was tanta-
> mount to owning it forever . . . Turning the pages,
> he had them all before him, at his command, af-
> fecting and ordering the plentitude of things that
> were. In reality, everything about birds gave rise
> to unease. Was it enough, he wondered, to verify
> their existence? The way the light modulated their
> feathers in flight, the warm, yellow flesh lining the
> bills of the young feeding in deeply sequestered
> nests, suffused him with a feeling of communion.
> Yet, for many, they were little more than a mobile
> decoration, scarcely worthy of scrutiny . . .

Like the boy in Page's poem, Thomas is "suffused
. . . with a feeling of communion" near bird nests, but
otherwise his responses to nature are far more jum-
bled, and complicated by self-consciousness. It's hard
to imagine the boy of "Only Child" even knowing
how to hold a gun, let alone using gulls and herons
for target practice. Are his unnaming, harmless detachment and his deep-in-the-grass reveries, then,
more praiseworthy than what Thomas does? Why do
they still seem to me sadly half-hearted alternatives to
the pleasure Thomas finds in power?

11

Naming, or what naming symbolizes, *can* hurt. Think of Page's finely woven tapestry-of-words "Portrait of Marina," in which a domineering father names his "pale spinster daughter" Marina in hopes that the name will "make her a water woman, rich with bells." Instead, for her "the name Marina meant / he held his furious needle for her thin / fingers to thread again with more blue wool / to sew the ocean of his memory." The father discourages the daughter from having an independent life, and her name itself becomes like a straitjacket, confining her to the roles he chooses for her.

12

In her glosa "A Bagatelle," Page enumerates species in a garden, including "Camellia: curiously, named for George J. Kamel, / Moravian, a Jesuit missioner." If Page is amused by such naming, A.S. Byatt is too, but more satirically. In her novella *Morpho Eugenia*, an English naturalist of lower-class background returns to his native country after a decade exploring the Amazon. While one character is thankful to names for freeing her imagination to write a book of fantasy – she finds herself "dragged along willy-nilly – by the language, you know – through Sphinx and Morpheus . . . – I suppose my Hermes was Linnaeus" – Byatt also pokes fun at a particularly proud sort of naming. The aging patriarch Harald Alabaster hopes in vain that "some monstrous toad or savage-seeming beetle in the jungle floor might immortalize me – *Bufo ama-*

zoniensis haraldii – Cheops nigrissimum alabastri – ."
Before leaving for the Amazon, the lower-class Adamson had a dream of rising in the world: "There would be a new species of ants, to be named perhaps *adamsonii,* there would be space for a butcher's son to achieve greatness." But once he starts to live in that distant foreign land, Adamson finds himself overwhelmed in "this green world of vast waste, murderous growth, and lazily aimless mere existence," and he records "his determination to survive, whilst comparing himself to a dancing midge in a collecting bottle."

Touché. The naturalist has become a bit of nature, the explorer an object, the bottler a bottled specimen.

13

Sometimes in Page's poems the radically transforming and transfigured are supreme, and the inner worlds we create are set higher than the sensuous worlds we're given. "Chinese Boxes" imagines a set of boxes diminishing in size until one reaches "an all-ways turning eye," an "inner eye / which sees the absolute / in emptiness." In her remarkable sestina "After Reading Albino Pheasants," Page is tugged between the beauties of the given physical world and the powers of a super-transforming eye. She wonders "Why would I wish to escape this world?" and acknowledges the shaping effects of heritage and environment, but near the end she speaks of "my truth" and "its own world / which is one part matter, nine parts imagination." She goes on: "I fear flesh which blocks imagination." In "Traveller, Conjuror, Journeyman" she writes:

> At times I seem to be attempting to copy exactly something which exists in a dimension where worldly senses are inadequate . . . Without magic the world is not to be borne.

An especially clear example: "After Donne" expresses frustration at the attractions and temptations of worldly senses. "For the least moving speck / I neglect God and all his angels," the poet complains. She is "subject to every tic and toc." Like a fervently other-worldly monk intent on the inner life and cautious of nature's superficialities, the poet there seems uneasy with the distractions of nature outside the life of the imagination.

In contrast to the flesh-and-blood birds of "Finches Feeding" or *Brazilian Journal* are the spiritual birds, horses, and indefinable beings of "Invisible Presences Fill the Air." And yet – a winning twist – for all their mysteriousness, these invisible presences too need names: "O who can name me their secret names? / Anael, opener of gates. / Phorlakh, Nisroc, Heiglot, / Zlar."

14

Why can't I rest easy with the line "one part matter, nine parts imagination"? Is it because I'd make the balance much more equal, or even tip it in favour of "matter," the raw material without which nothing would exist, our cradle and our continuing lifeblood and ground? Though Wordsworth's *The Prelude* sometimes seems to fill my consciousness with light as few other poems do, I have special qualms about these lines from its ending: "the mind of man becomes / A thousand times more beautiful than the earth / On which he dwells." The debate over the primacy of "Imagination or Nature" in Wordsworth remains dizzying and torturous. But, at least in isolation, lines like the above make me feel incomplete and in shock, as if I were abruptly cut adrift from much that I love. *A thousand times more beautiful*?

Our arrogant, short-sighted habits of desecrating the earth also make it hard for me to respond to the metaphors in Page's glosa "Planet Earth." While the poem seems written out of a desire to treat the earth carefully and reverently, Page doesn't question the metaphors from the four key lines of Neruda – the earth as something to be "spread out" and lovingly "ironed" – and her own lines compare the earth to a laundress's linens, a mother's child, a tapestry, gold leaf, a brass object in need of polishing. In the 1991 NFB documentary about her, Page spoke of the environmental crisis as "bigger than any war we've ever thought about." "Planet Earth" is more a poem of praise than a poem of polemics. Still, is making metaphors of the earth as our laundry and our child the way to change our thinking or the way to praise (or would it make more sense to see ourselves as laundry and children?).

Page's "Leather Jacket," on the other hand, protests with a purity that is bound to overwhelm any commentary on it. Its epigram comes from a medieval writer, Suhrawardi: "One day the King laid hold of one of the peacocks and gave orders that he should be sewn up in a leather jacket." Four stanzas into the poem, hard-to-bear sorrow and lament intensify:

Cry, cry for the peacock
hidden in heavy leather . . .

The peacock sees nothing
smells nothing
hears nothing at all
remembers nothing
but a terrible yearning
a hurt beyond bearing
an almost memory
of a fan of feathers
a growing garden

and sunshine falling
as light as pollen.

This peacock can be interpreted more as a symbol of self and beauty than as a species of bird; one critic, noting the role of the peacock in Sufism, has read its fate in Page's poem as "a metaphor for human entrapment," and Page herself has spoken of it as "a creative force blocked, arrested in some way." Thinking of the later poem "Planet Earth," I can also experience "Leather Jacket" as a sharply focussed yet multi-faceted poem partly about our vicious uses of other species, a poem that goes on haunting like an appall-

ing and guilt-exposing dream risen from the unconscious.

15

No, Page doesn't stay with conjured creatures, magical supra-senses, invisible presences, or secret names.
Within her work, *Brazilian Journal* is the most over-
flowing and detailed contrast to her poems of inner
vision. If her Brazilian experiences presented Page
with phantasmagoric possibilities, the phantasmago-
ria was usually that of intensified everyday reality. In
her poetry, too, the earthly often appears alongside
the "visionary"; and sometimes the borders between
the two seem to dissolve, and the distinction is very
imperfect. In *The Glass Air: Selected Poems* next to
the invisible presences poem, Page placed "Visitants,"
a poem about that most familiar bird, the pigeon. The
poem doesn't change the pigeons into doves of peace
or spirits; in the oaks they "stamp about like policemen," they are "voracious, gang-despoilers of the
tree-tops." In the last line, after the birds vanish, the
human witnesses are "left hungry in this wingless
hush," and in retrospect the appearance of the pigeons seems more magical than banal. Still, "Visitants" remains a poem obviously different from
"Invisible Presences," and a dialogue between the two
creates a denser field of meanings than either could
create on its own.

Imagine another dialogue, between "After Reading Albino Pheasants" and the much simpler, shorter
poem following it in *The Glass Air*. "Star-Gazer" sees

the "galaxy / italicized," and says "I have proof-read / and proof-read / the beautiful script." The final conclusion is: "There are no / errors." After the uncertainty, questioning, and efforts to defend imagination in "After Reading," this short poem may appear to be little but a declaration of the inherent rightness of nature, its unimprovable integrity as 100% matter. But Page's poem doesn't follow Dickinson's "811" in insisting that nature lies beyond language; it uses the convention of a "script" out there, and calls the poet a proof-reader. Complexities around the poem arise from questions like *Who is the poet to "proof-read" nature? How is she to declare it's error-free? Is the "script" perfect gibberish, or a perfect message, or something in between?*

16

"The Names of the Hare" is an anonymous Middle English poem modernized by Seamus Heaney. It includes what must be one of the most explosively adventurous lists in all poetry, a list composed of names for only one creature. If the author of the poem is anonymous, the hare is hardly that: Heaney's translation gives seventy-three names, including: "The stubble-stag, the long lugs, the stook-deer, the frisky legs, the wild one, the skipper, the hug-the-ground, the lurker, the race-the-wind, the skiver, the shag-the-hare, the hedge-squatter, the dew-hammer, the dew-hopper, the sit-tight, the grass-bounder, the jig-foot, the earth-sitter . . ."

Such varied naming hardly belongs only to Middle English poetry. Outside of poetry, just as species have regional variants, so do their names. In some cases, different names are used even in one area. For as long as I can remember I've heard the same bird referred to as Canada jay, grey jay, whiskey jack, and moose-bird. Such choices are healthy reminders that a name may be tentative, local, or random, and remains a far cry from identity.

My grandmother was a birdwatcher who encouraged my first birdwatching, but I don't recall ever feeling a need to pit her identification of species against an emotional appreciation of avian beauties and energies. She owned a copy of the 1917 magnum opus *Birds of America,* general editor T. Gilbert Pearson and consulting editor John Burroughs. One of the most engrossing, entertaining aspects of that book is its listing of "Other names," which reaches a comic plentitude that might've pleased the Joyce of *Finnegans Wake.* The surf scoter, for instance, has been known as spectacle coot, blossom-billed coot, horse-head, patch-head, skunk-head, plaster-bill, morocco-jaw, goggle-nose, and snuff-taker; the woodcock, as blind snipe, big-eyes, night partridge, night peck, timber doodle, hookum pake, labrador twister, and bogsucker. And Pearson lists an astonishing sixty-one alternative names for the ruddy duck, including dumpling duck, deaf duck, fool duck, sleepy duck, tough-head, hickory-head, stiff-tail, stick-tail, sprig-tail, leather-back, lightwood-knot, paddy-whack, shot-pouch, stub-and-twist, and blatherskite.

" . . . for sure the kittiwake."

kittiwake = tarrock, pick-me-up, coddy-moddy.

17

The names in "The Names of the Hare" conclude with "the creature no one dares to name" – this, after seventy-two alternative names! The poem appeals partly to a hunter's perspective. It begins by stating that a man "will never be the better" of the hare unless he first lay down his staff or bow and "with this litany / with devotion and sincerity / . . . sing the praises of the hare." At the end, the hare itself is addressed with the wish that it "come to me dead / in either onion broth or bread," so it may seem that all the naming has only served as a hunter's ploy, even if the overall effect of the naming has been to celebrate the animal. There's no denying the facts of death and carnivorous hunger in the poem's final lines, and thus the poem keeps from being *simply* a song of praise. Anon. has brought together into one rich broth the glory and harmfulness of naming, its potential for description and blessing and its involvement in destruction and death.

18

"Birds were his element like air and not / her words for them –making them statues / setting them apart . . ." Do words lose some of their Gorgon nature, have less ability to turn things into statues, when they vie with many other names to refer to the same thing? Is a label less a label when it's only one of many labels for the same thing? In one sense, yes, because the variety reminds us how ephemeral and local a name can be. But in another sense, no.

The mention of *Finnegans Wake* was a dead give-away. I revel in the names listed in the Pearson book like a kid rolling in a pile of leaves or a Canadian tourist partying in the streets of Rio at Carnival time. Then I shouldn't forget that, admiring and amused by a human facility, I've experienced intoxication by names much more than appreciation of whatever avian details helped inspire the linguistic carnival. The names are then like gigantic sign-posts next to a nesting sparrow.

19

After the carnival, time for a more skeptical period. A deep distrust of naming, in the Judaeo-Christian tradition, has often been linked to idolatry. God gets defined as beyond definition and naming, his name sometimes forbidden on human tongues or written out deliberately incomplete, as "G-d" or some such form. In our country, nobody has offered a more intelligent and generous-spirited amplification of this attitude than Tim Lilburn. In his essays and in his poetry collection *Moosewood Sandhills,* ex-Jesuit Lilburn dramatizes the need to swing constantly between adopting names and cancelling them. In his eyes, claims of knowing another species, of having the deer live "under its name," are forever false. In a TV documentary about him, Lilburn has said that the quality of "infinitude" traditionally applied to God actually belongs to all natural phenomena, each blade of grass, things complex far beyond our possible comprehension. As Lilburn writes in one of his essays: "behind these names, this veneer of intelligibility . . . that's where things live." In that light, we have to admit that a name – though sometimes it's all we have to start with – is a paltry thing compared to the unfathomable, never – half-perceived richness of what it points to.

20

Another danger of distinguishing and naming is that when they're pursued excessively the forest is lost for the trees, the ocean for the fish, the bird for its feathers. Page says in "This Frieze of Birds":

> . . . Rigidity supplies
> a just delineation
> of separates, divides
> crest, pinions, claws and eyes.
> No whole divides such rout.

In *The Tree,* Fowles warns of excessive hairsplitting that distracts us "from the total experience and total meaning of nature." He mentions a Victorian naturalist who studied twenty specimens of Dorset ferns that experts since have decided belong to only three species. The Victorian gent gave "each specimen some new sub-specific or varietal rank, as if they were unbaptized children and might all go to hell if they were not given individual names." (And yet, comically dogged and misled as the fern man may have been, I suspect there could be something oddly touch-

ing in him if his naming grew from an alertness to
uniqueness, a desire to recognize what was individual
about each specimen, not just each species.)

This road leads to the final stanza of Page's "After
Rain":

> And choir me too to keep my heart a size
> larger than seeing, unseduced by each
> bright glimpse of beauty striking like a bell,
> so that the whole may toll,
> its meaning shine
> clear of the myriad images that still –
> do what I will – encumber its pure line.

While these lines speak mostly in defence of the
whole, they see the glimpses as bright, beautiful,
seductive, not dull, cold, unattractive. At the end of
the poem, for all the celebration of the "whole," I
can't forget the many attractions described in the
poem's earlier stanzas, including "glorious chloro-
phyll" and after-rain snails making "broderie anglaise
from the cabbages, / chantilly from the choux-fleurs,
tiny veils." The poet herself admits that, whatever she
does to keep the whole pure, the reckless impurities
of "myriad images" remain in her mind.

21

In *Brazilian Journal,* Page writes one day in February
1959:

> I am working on a very large canvas which will
> probably be called *Woman's Room.* Funny how

some works demand titles – in fact, the whole business of naming is curious. A person you don't know
– one you see on the street, for instance – is quite
complete without a name. Looking at him I may
register his beauty or lack of it, his manner of dress-
ing, his possible employment . . . but once you
know a person, he *has* to have a name. He is incomplete without it.

Here Page suggests a commonsensically *practical* aspect to naming, our need for it if we want to go
beyond fleeting encounters and passing glances.

When parents name their child, are they only
trying to "own" it, or also trying to find an easy way
of referring to it beyond "our child"? I could accept
Fowles's statement that "Naming things is always
implicitly categorizing them and therefore collecting
them, attempting to own them" only with one large
qualification: that a name can also be a sign of interest, a form of recognition, an element of respect. In
my experience, people who don't know names for
things in nature or care to learn them often simply
don't see, hear, or otherwise notice the thing. When
I hear a dark throaty rough-edged call in the woods
and think "raven," the experience of hearing is vivi-
fied by having the name with which to picture the
bird, from times when I have seen it. Sometimes I've
found myself involuntarily saying "song sparrow,"
"nuthatch," or "raven" and surprised friends who
then say they've heard nothing. If recalling a name
can be a sort of possessive act, or a flaunting of
knowledge – some birders savour lists and statistics as

much as some baseball fans – it can be much more than that. When a bird is heard but not seen, knowing the name helps bring an image of the bird to mind and lets you feel piercingly the proximity of another being, or even silently send off a kind of mental greeting to it, a feeling of gratitude simply that it is there. When I hear a faint blurry nasal honk and think "nuthatch," I find it hard to agree with Hegel that by naming the animals in the Garden of Eden Adam "annihilated them in their existence as beings." A Robert Hass poems speaks of this notion that "a word is elegy to what it signifies." If words can be bombs, erasers, or subtractors, can't they also be pencils, pointers, gestures? Here's an alternative Eden myth: Adam named the beasts only when he began to see them, hear them, feel curious about them, and recognize them as fellow species. While exploitation would follow, that initial naming was a way of bringing images of animals into human consciousness, while recognizing the animals' existence beyond it.

22

But sometimes isn't "pointer" or "gesture" too neutral and innocuous to be accurate? We read of the explorer James Cook without thinking of cooking, kitchens, and stoves, but Page's poem "Cook's Mountains" is one of the clearest poems anywhere to show how a name for a thing can get inextricably balled up in our ways of perceiving it. Cook named a range in Australia "the Glass House Mountains." The poet

relates how when a driver told her the name her view
of the mountains was forever changed:

> And instantly they altered to become
> the sum of shape and name.
> Two strangenesses united into one
> more strange than either.
> Neither of us now
> remembers how they looked before they broke
> the light to fragments as the driver spoke.

In these lines Page doesn't seem to bemoan the effects
of naming upon perception; Cook's naming isn't
obviously seen as destructive or regrettable. She ac-
cepts the "Two strangenesses united into one," or
even admires them. But earlier and later in the poem,
there's a subtly unsettling emphasis on the human
vision of the landscape. The poem begins:

> By naming them he made them.
> They were there
> before he came
> but they were not the same.
> It was his gaze
> that glazed each one.
> He saw
> the Glass House Mountains in his glass.
> They shone.

The very first line can be read as startlingly abrupt,
suggesting a violent overthrow of what the mountains
were in themselves before Cook arrived. Then right
away the poem undercuts too strict a belief in its first

line by admitting that the mountains were there before their English observer, even if his naming would
change later English viewers' experience of them
(Aboriginal names for the mountains lie outside the
scope of the poem; if the poem or one like it were
written today, it might implicitly acknowledge the
politics of disparate naming, the question of which
and whose names prevail.) Page herself later continues the act of seeking out metaphors for the landscape
–"Like mounds of mica, / hive-shaped hothouses, /
mountains of mirrors glimmering" – and ends not
with further views of the mountains but with an image
of Cook "upon a deck / his tongue / silvered with
paradox and metaphor." The mention of "Queens-
land" reminds us of the title; both it and "Cook's
Mountains" are terms of ownership, like flags stuck
in a landscape. Page's poem is hardly a poem of
condemnation or protest, but with illuminating delicacy it encompasses both our marvelling over a union
of place and name, and our questioning about what's
lost in the process of naming.

23

So what happens to the unnamed son, the boy indifferent to naming and prone to dreamy reveries and
feelings of kinship with birds, when he grows up? The
poem concludes:

> Like every mother's boy he loved and hated
> smudging the future photograph she had,
> yet struggled within the frames of her eyes and then

froze for her, the noted naturalist –
her very affectionate and famous son.
But when most surely in her grasp, his smile
darting and enfolding her, his words:
"Without my mother's help . . . " the dream
    occurred.

Dozens of flying things surrounded him
on a green terrace in the sun
and one by one
as if he held caresses in his palm
he caught them all and snapped and wrung their
    necks
brittle as little sticks.
Then through the bald, unfeathered air
and coldly as a man could walk
against a metal backdrop, he
bore down on her
and placed them in her wide maternal lap
and accurately said their names aloud:
woodpecker, sparrow, meadowlark, nuthatch.

In the brutal clarity of these lines, there's some sharp
psychological sketching. Below its surface, the poem
is ambiguous about how much active, domineering
control the mother actually wielded over the boy. It's
possible that he's driven less by her manipulations
than by the guilt nagging inside himself; her "grasp"
may be a grasp he feels more than she exerts. In one
of the hardest ironies of the poem, he "froze for her,"
as if he suffered the same fate he imagined the birds
suffering when her names threatened to turn them
into statues.

    The concluding nightmare brings back, in the

famous adult, all the child's resentment. It would be wrong, I think, to say that in the dream the mother gets her just desserts and is shown the error of her ways, the murderous neck-wringing implicit in naming. We can hardly escape thoughts of a neurotic reliance of the son on his mother, a weakness in him that thwarts him from a deeper selfhood, his inability or unwillingness to realize something between the extremes of dry, spiritless taxonomy and a dreamy experience of nature that may show more detachment than engagement. Rather than presenting an anti-scientific view that naming merely kills, Page has written a packed- with-implication narrative that dramatizes two questionable approaches to nature, and leaves a more genuinely caring and enthusiastic approach in the wings. Such an approach emerges in other poems, and in *Brazilian Journal* with all the brilliance of a peacock's tail or a toucan's feathers.

24

Write a poem called "The Names of the Ruddy Duck," but with no hunter's soup at the end. Or write a glosa based on these four lines from "Cook's Mountains":

> And instantly they altered to become
> the sum of shape and name.
> Two strangenesses united into one
> more strange than either.

But "united into one" trips you up, because what is named keeps its separateness, its intransigence, its uncapturable "it"-ness. The debate goes on. A name is a hand, a cage, a bridge, a brand, a window.

THE HIDDEN ROOM

Collected Poems by P.K. Page

SUSAN MUSGRAVE

"Nobody ever came back to bed because of a poem," wrote Anselm Hollo. "Poetry makes nothing happen," said W.H. Auden. But once in a while you read a poem you would hop into bed for – a poem that makes something happen, and forever changes the way you move through your life, and see the world.

P.K. Page's poem, "Stefan," short enough to quote in its entirety, is a poem that changed my way of thinking – about thought:

> Stefan
> aged eleven
> looked at the baby and said
> "When he thinks it must be pure thought
> because he hasn't any words yet"
> and we
> proud parents
> admiring friends
> who had looked at the baby
>
> looked at the baby again.

P.K. Page writes "pure poetry," that is, poetry unencumbered by the freight of biography or gossip, poems that don't invite speculation about the poet or her personae, but arise from a bigger sense of the world, and our more universal concerns. To read her work is to discover ourselves wandering in a garden, after rain, where, "The snails have made a garden of green lace: / broderie anglaise from the cabbages, / Chantilly from the choux-fleurs, tiny veils," or through the halls of a dying nursing home where the elderly, beyond the pale of our words, pull themselves along with sticks and handrails ("Where are they going / these voyagers? Who steers?"), and laughing, often, at our own faces reflected in the polish of her words, the way a skinny black girl polishing the silver in a Brazilian house laughs to see her face appear in a tray.

The Hidden Room gives us the essential Page, two volumes gathered from over five decades, constituting a lot more than any ordinary Collected Poems. Readers will find poems from all Page's books, from *Unit of Fire* (1944) to *Hologram* (1994), a collection of glosas, together with many uncollected and hot-off-the-press poems, too.

That P.K. Page is fascinated with language, and what is hidden within words, behind words, is evident, but one suspects that her fascination is reciprocated, that language, too, is fascinated by P.K. Page. Her poetry has a strong visual aspect, which is hardly surprising since she is a painter as well, and there are times when her poems – like those of the great T'ang masters, George Woodcock suggests – read like those favourite paintings we own in which there is always

more to be discovered. Hers is the fertile green country of the imagination, with poems heavy as the
whiteness of snow. In "Stories of Snow," a national
treasure of a poem you could truly weep for, she
writes:

> In countries where the leaves are large as hands
> where flowers protrude their fleshy chins
> and call their colours
> an imaginary snowstorm sometimes falls
> among the lilies.
> And in the early morning one will waken
> to think the glowing linen of his pillow
> a northern drift, will find himself mistaken
> and lie back weeping.

There are poems in *The Hidden Room* not only worth
coming back to bed for, but that keep you awake at
night with their haunting imagery, poems such as
"Leather Jacket," prefaced with a quote from
Suhrawardi: "One day the King laid hold on one of
the peacocks and gave orders that he should be sewn
up in a leather jacket." P.K. Page describes the peacock, "a prisoner / that many-eyed bird / blind . . . "

> Enclosed in a huge leather purse.
> Locked in darkness.
> All its pupils sealed
> its tiny brain sealed
> its light and fluttering heart
> heavy as a plum.

She is able to make us feel, too, the peacock's "terrible

yearning / a hurt beyond bearing" in a growing garden with "sunshine falling / as light as pollen."

I believed I'd had an original, pure thought, at the beginning of this review when I started out by saying P.K. Page writes "pure poetry" but looking over the dustjacket to make sure I hadn't left out anything crucial, I found Northrop Frye's assessment of P.K. Page's poetry: "If there is such a thing as "pure poetry," this must be it; a lively mind seizing on almost any experience and turning it into witty verse . . . "

Indeed, there is a mischievous quality, a linguistic playfulness, to much of P.K. Page's work; she's not the sort of enemy you'd want to be tied to in a three-legged race, or appear in front of wearing the wrong hat. In "Truce" she writes:

My enemy in a purple hat
looks suddenly like a plum
and I am dumb with wonder
at the thought
of feuding with a fruit.

Feuding aside, she's a poet with great empathy for humanity. Her poems reach, always, for the light in darkness; in this sense they are moral poems, as defined by John Gardner who says writers have a moral obligation to the world to make their poetry and their fiction, ultimately, life affirming. P.K. Page has the ability to tackle weighty subjects – everything from the death of friends, to the way we should love

this planet earth – and still offer hope for the human
condition.

    It has to be loved the way a laundress loves her
        linens,
    the way she moves her hands caressing the fine
        muslins
    knowing their warp and woof,
    like a lover coaxing, or a mother praising.
    It has to be loved as if it were embroidered
    with flowers and birds and two joined hearts upon
        it.
    It has to be stretched and stroked.
    It has to be celebrated.
    O this great beloved world and all the creatures in it.
    It has to be spread out, the skin of this planet.

HOLOGRAM DIMENSIONS

The poetry of P. K. Page.

TRAVIS LANE

P. K. Page's beautiful poems have made her among our most revered Canadian poets. It may be the cast of mind that shapes her poetry that makes her work distinctive. The world of nature and human society figures as images in Page's poetry, but rarely as matters of primary interest, and almost never as matters for investigation. Whether describing a garden, an office, or a migraine, Page's primary impulse is to shape the poem toward beauty – stylizing, exaggerating, with gorgeous effect – rather than to emphasize the mundane particularities of her subjects. The vitality of the poems derives both from the energy of Page's imagination and from the life force she perceives at work in, but to a very large degree veiled or shut out by, the bias and circumscription of the particular, of subjective experience, of the imperfect material world.

Page's most often repeated themes, that circumscription or enclosure is the characteristic of the life lived on the materialist plane, and that the subjective viewpoint is necessarily biased, inadequate, superficial – circumscribed – are not dissimilar to postmodernist awareness of the circumscribedness and bias of the subjective, and consequent distrust of narrative. Such themes may partially account for the sympathy and ease with which we, influenced as we all are by postmodernist thought, can, in general, approach her work.

Page shares postmodernist understanding of the shaping effect of language, when she speaks of the change a different language, Portuguese, made of herself when she learned to speak it in Brazil. "Who am I, then, that language can so change me?" ("Questions and Images," 187) But, unlike postmodernists, Page assumes language refers to something outside itself; what is unusual is that Page also believes language can refer to something outside the material world. Perhaps, she implies neither the particular language nor the individual "me" are important: language, like self, like the material world, whether beautiful or tawdry, tends to be regarded in Page's poetry as somehow at once circumscribing and insubstantial:

> At times I seem to be attempting to copy exactly something which exists in a dimension where worldly senses are inadequate . . . words which lead to the very threshold of some thing, some place; veiled by a membrane at times translucent, never yet transparent, through which I long to be absorbed.
>
> "Traveller, Conjuror, Journeyman" (183).

Thus, for Page, the poem becomes a sort of hologram, translucent, but sourced from beyond. But a hologram has no inside. There is, throughout Page's beautiful and mind-catching poetry, one less dimension than we customarily find in poetry of equal or greater stature: interiority, on a material or personal plane. It is a dimension in which she does not appear to be all that interested.

Images of circumscription abound in Page's poetry, particularly where she is describing motion. Even where she does not portray enclosure, the motions she pictures are non-progressive: tremblings in place, circular dances, seasonal repetitions, migrations, spinnings, hoverings, return trips, and are, therefore, circumscribed in their general circularity or repetitivity. Several poems describe journeys out that return to their beginnings, circular journeys. Numerous poems specify and describe motions within enclosed spaces, such as glass globes, kaleidoscopes, webs, mazes, screens, lenses:

> The standard roses disciplined, the slow seasons,
> the altering moment – quivering, intense –
> spring into cameo focus and through his small
> aperture a microscopic vision
> is caught in the gelid lens:
> bright leaves and blossoms, static, bloom and fall
> in continuing and changeless violence.
>
> "Portrait"

Undoubtedly the most famous of Page's images of circumscribed motion are the prison images of "The Stenographers":

> . . . in their eyes I have seen
> the pin men of madness in marathon trim
> race round the track of the stadium pupil.

and "Arras":

> the spinning world is stuck upon its poles,
> the stillness points a bone at me, I fear
> the future on this arras . . .

In such poems the circumscription is a matter of material fate; the secretaries are confined by their jobs; the speaker in "Arras" fears she is somehow stuck in the unreal / but material web of appearances.

However a different sort of circumscription is represented in Page's poetry as desirable, as a method of breaking through the prison/web/arras. The poetic eye is urged to withdraw its attention from the mass of detail in the material world "in a backward journey" toward the tiniest point "thought could hold to" ("A Backward Journey"); or, less commonly, to withdraw its attention to detail by looking beyond detail, as in "Sphinx," where "Sibelius" looks beyond stars. In prayer poems such as "Spinning" the poet desires to be:

> centred as never otherwise. In stock-
> stillness, dizzying movement find,
> spinning a dot.

The purpose of such concentration is to reach "spaces

where / my Father's house has many dimensions"
("Spinning") but not, one gathers, material dimensions. Or, again, as Page says in "The Gold Sun":

> the way a mystic masters the mystique
> of making more by focusing on one
> until at length, all images are gone
> except the sun, the thing itself, deific,
> *and say this, this is the centre that I seek.*

Motion that is not in some sense circumscribed,
repetitive, or contained does not much appear in
Page. For in Page's poetry the exploration, interroga-
tion, or mapping of the material or subjective world
is not the point, except insofar as pattern or beauty
might be shown: "I am a traveller. I have a destination
but no maps," writes Page in "Traveller, Conjuror,
Journeyman" (184). Her compass leads to a spiritual
centre.

That the material world (however vividly described and celebrated) is in Page's poetry somehow
insubstantial is apparent even where the poems themselves do not specifically say so. For example, Page's
many poems which represent dreams appear to re-
gard the dream events as equivalent, in their materi-
ality (or immateriality), to the events of the waking
world: "so flies and blows the dream that haunts us
when we wake / to the unreality of bright days!" ("Cry
Ararat!")

There is, of course, a major difference between
the dream life and the waking life. The conscious
mind does not intervene or think as dream pro-

gresses; instead we move sluggishly or violently through our emotions and sensations, often in terms of our mythic subconsciousness. Perhaps, in Page, dreams are valued precisely because the ego, the waking mind, *is* absent.

> What, indeed, is this duologue, so like an effortless poem? Can projected images be manifested as dreams? Are all dreams projected? Or some? Is the Dreamer active or passive? Initiator or recipient? . . . And what about the waking Dreamer? Are thoughts the invisible dreams of a daylight world? Projected by what, or whom? Jung's collective unconscious? Rumi's angels?
>
>   "Traveller, Conjuror, Journeyman" (191)

Asleep, we are less our selves. Without that interfering ego, the dream approaches the condition of the Dreamer (if you like), or (if you'd rather) the condition of the unthinking natural world, in which we like Wordsworth's Lucy may be immersed. (This, of course, assumes that we do not believe, like the materialist Scrooge, that dreams are merely matters of underdone potato.)

The insubstantiality of Page's material, waking world is also apparent in the many poems Page has written about people and society. Her descriptions of people are stylized, mythologized, almost impersonal. (Is there any lovelier headache than the migraine of Marina, in "Portrait of Marina"? Yet what an abstract and stylized portrait!) Page's poems expressing social concern tend to employ Audenesque generalities, which (as they do also in Auden) seem to distance the poetic speaker from the objects of concern. Are menial office workers, *quite* as miserable, as "entrapped" as they appear in Page's several poems about them? I think it is a habit of generalizing for the sake of decorative metaphor that leads to these exaggerations. Page is as generalizing when writing about little girls or adolescents:

> A shoal of them in a room makes it a pool.
> How can one teacher keep the water out,
> or, being adult, find the springs and taps
> of their tempers and tortures?
> Who, on a field filled with their female cries
> can reel them in on a line of words
> or land them neatly in a net?
> On the dry ground they goggle, flounder, flap.
>
> "Young Girls"

These little girls are no more realistic than Page's typists, policemen, landladies . . . Even the character Cullen, who can be read as a figure for the poet herself, is stylized, more of a dream figure than a biographical account. Such stylization may be related to Page's desire to eliminate as much as possible from her verse the tyrannies of subjectivity, individuality, and ego. By stylizing, exaggerating, de-individualizing, she mythologizes. Her "people" become, all of them, figures on an arras.

Page's love poetry, too, can seem exaggerated to the point of impersonality. Some of the love poems are so extravagantly expressed, as if anxious to lose

the ego in the process of Ideal Love, that they scant
the more moderate pleasures of personal domesticity.
Even her charming domestic vignettes, celebrating
the beauty of transitory moments, avoid the self-be-
trayals and the unwanted confidences we associate
with the over-intimate.

In her *Brazilian Journal,* Page quotes Schweitzer
in a way which throws light on Page's own attitudes:

> No one should compel himself to show to others
> more of his inner life than he feels it natural to
> show. We can do no more than let others judge
> for themselves what we inwardly and really are,
> and do the same ourselves with them. The one es-
> sential thing is that we strive to have light in our-
> selves . . . In general, how much I suffered through
> so many people assuming the right to tear open
> all the doors and shutters of my inner self!
>
> *Brazilian Journal* (210)

Page's instinct for privacy does not mean, however,
that her love poems can not be deeply moving; some
of them, on the subject of loss, such as "The End,"
are heart-rending. But they are not personal. Related
to Page's dislike of the intrusive ego is her avoidance
of argument or sustained narrative. Page's poems are
definitely not made up out of a quarrel with her self.
Curiosity about her self, or about others' selves, seems
inhibited; whether by a concern for privacies, or by
lack of poetic interest. (Which is not to say a lack of
personal interest; how one chooses to conduct one's
poetry is no sign of how one chooses to conduct one's

life.) As Page remarks in her *Brazilian Journal,* "Strange how I rarely write of things that distress me. Why? Because I can not bear it? Because I try to forget? (I don't succeed.)" (l94). This moment of self-observation expressed is extremely rare in Page's work, and it occurs in a journal, not a poem.

Nor does Page usually write as if inclined to persuade us, the readers, as instructor, confidant, or friend. Indeed the reader does not generally figure in Page's poetry; in general, with some exceptions, we overhear rather than are addressed:

> I truly think I do not write or draw for you or you or you . . . Attention excludes you. You do not exist. I am conscious only of being "hot" or "cold" in relation to some unseen centre.
> "Traveller, Conjuror, Journeyman" (184)

(One can not fairly count the poems addressed to the dead or unhearing as personally engaged with the reader.) And, with the exception of the Frostian "Address at Simon Fraser," Page's poems are not primarily concerned with the analysis of events or the development of ideas. Ideas, like narrative, are things of the material world; effective tools where they belong and in context, which, for Page, would appear to be prose.

The poem, for Page, as we have seen, would appear to be largely a spiritual endeavour, or at the very least, a matter of the construction of something elegant, beautiful. Increasingly, as her work matures, she emphasizes the spiritual values:

My subconscious evidently knew something about
the tyranny of subjectivity years ago when it de-
sired to go "through to the area behind the
eyes/where silent, unrefractive whiteness lies."
>   "Traveller, Conjuror, Journeyman" (191).

That unrefractive whiteness is, for Page, the Projector, the Dreamer, the Life Force. With different
intentions and perceptions than those of the postmodernist, Page comes, like the postmodernist, to
prefer process to artifact. On piecing together a
poem, she explains:

> it is the search that matters. When the final piece
> slips into place the finished poem seems no more
> important than the image in a completed jigsaw
> puzzle.
>   "Traveller, Conjuror, Journeyman" (185).

Page goes on to add that a completed painting or a
completed poem are "worth little more than a passing glance . . . They are alternate roads to silences."
Poems and paintings for Page should not be excur-
sions into the ordinary, the personal, the subjective.
Because:

> He belongs to the sea – we all do. We are part of its
>   swell.
> And only the shoreline grounds us. Yet we stand
> hands tied, deluded, seemingly earthbound
> imagining we belong to the land
> which is only a way-station, after all.
> We are the sea's, and as such we are at its beck.

We are the water within the wave and the wave's
    form.
And little will man – or woman, come to that –
know what he shall dream when drawn by the sea's
    wrack
or what he shall hope for once it is clear that
he'll never go back.

                    "The End"

We do not really belong, (being "half-angel," as she
says in "Address at Simon Fraser"), to what is "only
a way-station," the insignificant land, the flawed,
circumscribing "material":

All crippled. All with flaws.
You, me
the wheeling young
buds blind on their stalks
eggs in their nest
sealed from the sun.

                 "Your Hand Once"

Our destination, our interests, should be other. Perhaps a work of art might "re-align us – all our
molecules / to make us whole again" or "vivify /
Plato's invisible reality" ("Address at Simon Fraser").
What we should want, is, as Page says in "Another
Space," that the "glass partition" melt, so that our
enclosed vision, which has been "in stasis locked"
should now show "a new direction," so that we can
enter the hologram of appearances and become one
with Projector of Light, the Life Force.

ENTRANCED

A Conversation with P.K. Page

LUCY BASHFORD AND JAY RUZESKY

The following interview is a blend of two conversations which took place at P.K. Page's home in Victoria, B.C. in the summer of 1996 and the fall of 1999.

L.B. & J.R.: In the introduction to *Hologram* you explain what a glosa is and you mention the difference between "affinity with" and "influence." I think the idea of finding one's voice is a false construct. It's like developing a personality or something. You have one. It's there. I like your analogy of birds brought up in isolation. They take from the songs of others to complete their species-song.

P.K. PAGE: It's a fascinating analogy, isn't it? I read it in an article in the *New Yorker* and it seems to apply in many areas. What could you learn in isolation? Not much.

L.B. & J.R.: But what you would take coming out of isolation is what was already yours.

P.K. PAGE: We're not thieves. The voice is innate, if undeveloped.

L.B. & J.R.: Doris Lessing suggests that writers are a kind of organism, that we are connected by what we do. It struck me as I was reading the glosas that in this form you . . .

P.K. PAGE: . . . marry another writer.

L.B. & J.R.: Yes. Through the text, part of the writer becomes part of us. The connection that this form makes seems profound. Not only are you making the connection that usually occurs when you read and write, and have an affinity for someone, but you link with them and it's more like the two of you sitting down and writing together. You begin so obviously with their words.

P.K. PAGE: and their rhythm to some extent rubs off on you. Not entirely but to some extent. It's a funny feeling of intimacy when you're working with some-one else's lines. Lessing's idea that poets are all one being, as are all people of any similar discipline, fascinated me and I think that there is some very great truth in it. It's a very funny experience to use other people's lines. It's more than just writing a poem. It's merging. There were times when I wondered if I was just doing imitation Stevens or imitation Bishop.

L.B. & J.R.: You are merging and yet you are an individual at the same time. It's clear reading through *Hologram* that it's your book and these are your poems, and they're you.

P.K. PAGE: Well some of my best lines are not mine. I have to accept that. It was interesting to allow someone else's line to overshadow me. I don't mean that they can't and don't frequently, but when you juxtapose them it is quite obvious and you have to be prepared to say, "Alright, I'll take a back seat. That is the best line."

L.B. & J.R.: Are you thinking of one in particular?

P.K. PAGE: The Graves, actually. That extraordinary line of his: "Nor for the tall, eventual catafalque." I could never have dreamed that up in a hundred-thousand years.

L.B. & J.R.: That could easily be you!

P.K. PAGE: Of course you don't pick the four lines, do you, unless there's some strong affinity.

L.B. & J.R.: Your work is your path. And it seems that there are certain elements that have been there for you for a long time. In *Hologram* there are major insights. It's very powerful. In an essay that you wrote in 1970, "Traveller, Conjuror, Journeyman" *[The Glass Air],* you say that the "struggle is to fit the 'made' to the 'sensed' in such a way that the whole can occupy a world larger than the one I normally inhabit. This process involves scale. Poem or painting is by-product." The process is larger than the product of the poem. It's something you may not be able to see as clearly as someone outside of a book like *Hologram,* but the poems indicate a larger process going on behind the work.

P.K. PAGE: I had a period of quite astonishing clarity when I wrote that essay. I had, for a short time, a breakthrough into another understanding. It didn't last, but I have the residue of it still. I think I've always realized how little we know and had a sense that perhaps what we are seeing is the first layer of something more. But I can't articulate it because it belongs to another life, not the life of the senses.

L.B. & J.R.: There's a mystical element in your poems, a visionary quality. Do you know where they come from?

P.K. PAGE: I haven't any idea. But I do think that when I'm very concentrated in a poem, and I am more concentrated writing a set form than writing free verse – the focus is more intense. It's a very narrow focus but it isn't a shallow focus. When people ask me if I meditate I say, "No, I don't." But possibly I do meditate. Perhaps when I'm writing I'm meditating.

L.B. & J.R.: Is art an avenue into some more mystical place for you? What is it that opens doors? It's an odd thing to do to sit in a room alone and write.

P.K. PAGE: Some people would say it's nothing more than a form of egotism. That you think what you have to offer is so bloody important that you're prepared to shut yourself up and do it at the expense of all around you. Look at Rilke who begged his life through in order to write. And I've known other writers who thought that they should be kept, that being a poet was enough. Clearly it can be a form of ego. But in the case of Rilke, thank god for it. Although I don't think it was ego with him. And I've never felt it was ego with me. I don't see how anyone can get puffed up about how great they are because it seems to me that the artist is a channel. And I suppose the purer the channel – and by that I don't mean saintly but clearer – the clearer the channel the clearer what comes through. It never occurs to me that it has much to do with me and it never has. It doesn't matter whether it's a bad poem or a good poem. So I don't think it is ego. It's a process. And I'm never terribly interested in the thing when it's finished. People say, "O, aren't you thrilled to have the book in your hands?" The book is the by-product, the evidence of the fact that a lot of stuff went on. I think in our age the artists have let us down very badly. And when I say artists I mean whoever the creative members of society are. I include myself in this. With some exceptions, of course, I feel we have lost our sense of scale. I don't know – we seem as stuck in the "material" as any businessman.

L.B. & J.R.: We've been forced into making ourselves a "business." We're referred to as cultural industries. The tax system, all of that makes you start to think about it in a different way. We don't really have time to look in and beyond.

P.K. PAGE: Do we know how to get in? When you think of fiction today, there isn't much that has an extra dimension. There is some but much seems to have, in fact, anticipated the strictures imposed by voice appropriation and applied them widely. It presents too narrow a view and is not dissimilar to the confessional phase in poetry. I feel that until you can reach beyond the self, you haven't a great deal to say. It's as if we have taken a backwards step although maybe, for some unknown reason, we had to.

L.B. & J.R.: There's a connection between the economy and creativity.

P.K. PAGE: Writing poetry was never my livelihood. It was always something quite apart. I think I was lucky in that I grew up in a golden era. When we started *Preview* in Montreal in the 1940s we didn't have any money. There were no grants. Each of us put five dollars in the pot. For me that was a lot of money. I was earning eighty dollars a month. We cobbled the magazine together ourselves, very clumsily. I did most of the typing, and I was a bad typist. If any of us wrote something good, the others were always quick to say so and genuinely pleased. We felt it lifted the whole level for everybody, that it was like pouring sugar in tea. The whole of the cup was sweetened by it. I still feel my heart lift when I read something good and I want to tell the writer. But it's different today from the 1940s. Some other element seems to have crept into the world. People are more wrangly and I hate it. But I must admit I don't like it if someone I think is a bad writer gets a lot of praise.

L.B. & J.R.: But if that same person writes something brilliant . . .

P.K. PAGE: I honestly think I am pleased. It's the work, not the personality that matters.

L.B. & J.R.: You talk about recapturing and remembering. I'm wondering if recapturing might go beyond childhood memories to before we were born.

P.K. PAGE: I think it's a possibility. Just as I think it's a possibility that we may have chosen our parents and where we landed on earth. Because we measure time linearly we get locked into it. But there is another time that has nothing to do with linear time and I think I have known about it since I was quite young.

L.B. & J.R.: In a bookstore I saw a section called "miscellaneous spirituality" and I thought that would be a good shelf for you. There is a solid spiritual centre in your work that I wouldn't trace to any particular place. Sufism . . . but even that is a non-religion.

P.K. PAGE: Actually it claims to be the inner part or essence of every religion. It is also a body of knowledge which has been enormously enriching to me.

L.B. & J.R.: In another essay you say you'd like to be a magician. Part of being a magician is being observant so you can do things other people won't notice. There's a thin line between a visionary quality and a magical quality because magicians as we know them don't do real magic.

P.K. PAGE: I don't know that I'd say that I want to be a magician today. There's quite a lot of deception in it. The Sufis say that miracles do not fly in the face of laws. They only fly in the face of laws that we, at this stage, know of. Any miracle is part of a logical or illogical! construct but it isn't breaking laws, it's just in tune with higher laws that we can't possibly imagine. I wouldn't mind getting in touch with those higher laws.

L.B. & J.R.: I think that's what you're doing. *Hologram* is a powerful book because through your search you've reached some point where you're connected to something not everyone is. It's inspiring. There's a quotation at the back of Tim Lilburn's book, *Moosewood Sandhills* from Gregory of Nysa who says that "the desire to see God, is a vision of God." That's something that makes sense in terms of your work. Knowing that there are other places to go is a way of being there.

P.K. PAGE: That's a good quotation.

L.B. & J.R.: In the 1970 essay you ask the question, "What am I trying to do with my writing?" and the answer is "play" with a question mark. Are you still playing?

P.K. PAGE: I think so. It's very serious play. I get such pleasure out of just playing with the way words rhyme or don't rhyme. You know play can be intensely serious when you see a child sitting on the floor playing with bits of paper and an old tin can. With children it's almost as if they're in touch with another dimension.

L.B. & J.R.: And why do we lose that?

P.K. PAGE: Well, I suppose one has to get on with some very practical things in life. There are the dishes in the sink and they have to be done. There's all that business of keeping yourself clean and feeding yourself. Idries Shah, a Sufi teacher, says that once upon a time people played with toys. Now toys play with people. We seem to have allowed this material world to manipulate us, to take us over.

L.B. & J.R.: What was it like to go back over a life's work and have it collected in *The Hidden Room?* Were there any surprises?

P.K. PAGE: I don't think any real surprises. Although some of my very early work which didn't go in to *The Hidden Room* surprised me. My reach so exceeded my grasp. I was astonished to see what I was reaching for and failing to deliver because of inexperience and ineptitude. There was a very long poem about the sea as seen through the eyes of a sunbather on the beach and a fisherman who was coping with it as a reality. It surprised me because I wrote it when I was young and reaching out for something quite big and impossible. Some of the surprises were the poems that Stan Dragland included. I had put myself in Stan's hands pretty well, but retained the right to argue or dispute. Some of the early surrealist poetry I think I wouldn't have chosen myself.

L.B. & J.R.: There have been a number of comments about the ordering of *The Hidden Room.* People are troubled by the fact that it's not ordered chronologically. What do you think of that?

P.K. PAGE: I think first about the people who object to it. I think they've been academicized to death.

Many academics think chronologically but is it not possible for a body of work to have an organic whole that's not necessarily chronological? I think Stan found that organic whole. There is a related subject, one that I argued about repeatedly with Dorothy Livesay. She insisted that you shouldn't revise an early poem at a later date. My position was and is that it depends upon what you are trying to do. If you are trying to write the best poem you are capable of, then you can and must. My poetry, after all, is not very autobiographical.

L.B. & J.R.: Was there a lot of revision then for this book?

P.K. PAGE: Very little really. But I could have revised. It's my work!

L.B. & J.R.: You must have gone through chronologically when you were gathering the poems together for *The Hidden Room*. That's not something that one often does. How did it feel to go back?

P.K. PAGE: I could see very clearly how pelted with images I was when I was young. And then when I reached the point where I realized how little control I had over those images, I addressed the problem in the poem, "After Rain." I wasn't quite as pelted with images after that. The act of writing came through a slightly different filter. I had made a conscious choice and in doing that, I both gained and lost. I lost a certain spontaneity perhaps. I was also interested to see how extraordinarily romantic I was, romantic and idealistic.

L.B. & J.R.: Do you see big changes in your work? I can open the book anywhere and they seem like P.K. Page poems. The voice hasn't changed that much. Do you see that too?

P.K. PAGE: There's a certain ground, to use a musical term, that goes through it all. I think some of my rhythms were more interesting when I was young than they are now. Like this poem, "The Crow," which I wrote when I was really quite young:

> by the wave rising
> by the wave breaking
> high to low
> by the wave riding the air
> sweeping the high air low . . .

I don't think I could write that way now. I'm not talking about content, but my rhythmic form was more varied. Iambic has left its heavy foot on me, its elephant foot. One of the things that emerges from *The Hidden Room* is that even when I was young I wasn't writing about myself very much. It's one of the complaints I get now; that my poetry is too impersonal. And yet it always was. I was looking out. I was looking at the man with one small hand, or the old man in the garden, or the stenographers, typists. It wasn't often that I was looking at myself, although I suppose in some sense I was the man with the small hand, the old man in the garden, etcetera, etcetera.

L.B. & J.R.: Was that a part of the time?

P.K. PAGE: Oh, probably. The objective-correlative

of Eliot was my credo more or less, and the confessional poets hadn't hit the fan yet; it was a different period. And yet at the same time I think of Patrick Anderson whose work was very personal. But I am an observer, a watcher – always have been. There was a man in Ottawa who used to call me the "Seeing Eye bitch." He wasn't being rude about my being bitchy. He was a dog man. He said, "One has to be very careful around you because you see everything." And I did. At that period in my life when I was very observant. It wasn't critical observation; it was camera. And if you are looking out, then you write about what you see. I had been flung from the protected world in which I grew up to Montreal in wartime – a culture of two languages and sophisticated people. On my own. I was twenty-two. I was seeing many things I'd never seen before: stenographers, typists and the effect of the war on all these people. I was fascinated, utterly fascinated by it. And so, inevitably, I wanted to write about it. Even more than I wanted to write about what was going on inside me and plenty was, I can tell you.

L.B. & J.R.: You have an amazing vocabulary. I was reading Robert Enright's review of *The Hidden Room* and he said there's only one other person who can use "maculate" and that's T.S. Eliot.

P.K. PAGE: You know what it means don't you?

L.B. & J.R.: No.

P.K. PAGE: It means spotted. Dirty. Maculate . . . immaculate. It has a certain ambiguity. It can mean soiled, I suppose, but it can mean spotted. I used it in "Arras." It's the peacock's tail. To get back – I don't think my vocabulary's very big, but it may be quirky.

L.B. & J.R.: Again in your essay, "Traveller, Journeyman, Conjuror," you talk about being hot or cold when you're writing and I was wondering how you know when you're hot or cold?

P.K. PAGE: Do you remember a game in which your friends, while you were out of the room, chose an object in the room which you had to find. You were guided only by their telling you that you were getting hot, or getting cold. It's a feeling of proximity. In the game your friends gave you clues. But when you are writing some split part of you gives you the clues. It's as if there is a lode that draws you and when you get close to it you know you're hot. It's like a fire. There's some emanation. It doesn't necessarily mean you are writing well, unfortunately!

L.B. & J.R.: In the film version of one of your short stories you've suddenly become an actor. What was your experience of acting? Did elements of the performing you've done at public readings come into it or was it an entirely different thing?

P.K. PAGE: Maybe I should go back a little bit. When I was young I didn't know whether I wanted to act or write. I thought maybe I wanted to act. I had no experience of acting except in school plays and amateur theatre in the Maritimes and I loved it. I simply loved it. But I wasn't very good. It gradually dawned on me that I couldn't play Lady Macbeth and if you're

an actor you want to play Lady Macbeth. I realized I
hadn't the capacity and maybe I better stick to writing. But I fiddled around. I did some radio acting
when I was quite young. I had a boyfriend in radio
and I wrote a series of duologues that we performed.
I've always been interested in theatre. Film has never
captured my imagination in quite the way that theatre
has. I put the whole thing completely out of my head.
Then thirty years ago Barrie Maclean asked me to
play the principal role in a film he wanted to make
from one of my stories. I said, "Barrie, you need an
actor and I'm not an actor." "No, no," he said, "you
don't understand. You'd be right for it. Half of it's
camera work." I said "No, no, no," but anyhow
nothing came of it. Then, when Barrie died suddenly
last year, as a memorial to him, I agreed to play in
Anna Chernakova's version of the same movie, even
though I was too old for the role. I couldn't remember
lines. My memory was not as good. So they used
voice-over which I read in a studio and the only lines
I had to say on camera were small bits of dialogue,
many of which were spontaneous. I also knew I
couldn't act and had no idea what to do in front of
the camera. In the theatre you have a certain distance
from your audience and if you ham it isn't so notice-
able, but if the camera is in your face and you're
mugging . . . There are a lot of uncertainties and
unknowns. You never know which part of you the
camera is shooting. Are they shooting you entire, or
only your left elbow? You don't know. It's a funny
feeling. You become almost disembodied. Dismem-

bered is a better way to put it. Someone had said the less you act on film the better so most of the time I walked around with no expression on my face at all because I didn't really know what was expected of me. I was given very little direction. And it's boring! They shoot over and over again. You do the damn thing until you're fed up with it. Much of your spontaneity has gone by the time they're finally satisfied with the camera-angle or the lighting. Also it's collaborative. But I find working with people is always interesting, even as I say it was boring.

L.B. & J.R.: You wouldn't do it again?

P.K. PAGE: No. But once was interesting. I knew film was a great deal of fakery. After all, I had worked at the National Film Board at one time, and I certainly know to what extent it's fakery now. But what really disappointed me was how much of the story was lost in the filming.

L.B. & J.R.: You're involved in various collaborations. You're working on an oratorio?

P.K. PAGE: To celebrate Canadian Composers, Nicholas Goldschmidt dreamed up Music 2000, a Canada-wide festival of music. It began in Whitehorse on the night of the winter solstice and it will move across the country during the year. Lou Applebaum and Mavor Moore have written an opera based on Samuel Butler's Erewhon which will be performed in Victoria. And Derek Holman of Toronto has written an oratorio, "The Hidden Reality," using seven of my poems, one written especially for it. The score calls for the Toronto Symphony Orchestra, the Mendelssohn Choir, the Toronto Children's Chorus, and Ben Hepner, if you please! Among the soloists.

L.B. & J.R.: There are two other collaborations you've been involved in lately. One is the renga you did with Philip Stratford, "And Once More Saw the Stars," and the other is the exhibition of poems and drawings with Mimmo Paladino in which he took some of your writing and made drawings from them.

P.K. PAGE: The most intimate of all was the renga, because my mind was being changed by Philip and Philip's mind was being changed by mine. His mind would be going one direction and mine would jog him off course and vice versa. So it was very intimate. Although impersonal. The correspondence from this period is quite interesting. We used slow mail because he didn't have a fax, and our personal lives never entered into the correspondence at all. He went through a major operation in the middle of it. He never referred to it in any of his letters. There was a very long silence and I thought, "He's bored. This is it." I learned later that he'd been through surgery. But in our letters we began to know each other's minds. That was the closest collaboration. It wouldn't work with everyone. With Paladino there's no collaboration at all, if collaboration means working together. I've never met Paladino. I've never spoken to him. I've never written to him. He's never communicated with me. Francesca Valente, the director of the Istituto Italiano di Cultura, Toronto, gave him the poems that she translated into Italian and he came up with his images. It was the least personal collaboration of all. The most abstract really.

L.B. & J.R.: But your minds did meet in a distant way.

P.K. PAGE: I was in no way indifferent to the way his mind responded but I was not involved. I was interested in seeing what images he drew from my poems but I felt little connection to them. I loved some of the drawings. I'd give anything to own one of them. But they didn't seem to have much to do with me. What he picked from a poem was not the image I would have picked.

L.B. & J.R.: Your chapbook *Alphabetical* (Hawthorne Society 1998) won the 1999 bp Nichol Chapbook Award. It seems a change in direction for you. It's playful and also serious. Where did that poem come from?

P.K. PAGE: I wrote the word "afterwards" and it seemed to me that "afterwards" was a very funny word because you couldn't conceive of it if there hadn't been a "before." Then I thought, having written a little about afterwards, I'll write a little about "before." And then the whole alphabet seemed to unscroll before me. It amused me to write it and it came easily. And for me it is personal. My background is in it, my family. Bits of it are quite funny, I think.

L.B. & J.R.: PK, I get the sense that you're tying up loose ends, which is vaguely disturbing because you're . . .

P.K. PAGE: . . . getting ready for departure.

L.B. & J.R.: What I want to know is what some of those loose ends are.

P.K. PAGE: I am preparing for a further journey, there's no doubt about that. I'd like to get my affairs in order. Not to leave a mess for anyone else to deal with. I don't mean that I think I'm going to die tomorrow. I don't. I think I'm going to be here for a while. But there isn't a great deal of time left to do a lot of work in. One seems to be like a magnet in life and one accumulates, whether one wants to or not, an immense amount of matter. And I want to dispose of that. My final whack at controlling things. Also I have writing I want to do. I've got all my Mexican and Australian stuff, most of which may be useless except to a biographer. I'd like to get all my papers into some kind of shape. I don't see how one can help but think this way in one's eighties. But it's forward looking, going with the flow. It's not a closure. One book I want to do is the renga with the correspondence with Philip Stratford and an introduction by me and notes within the correspondence to indicate what was happening in Philip's life that slowed the renga down. We called it a renga but of course it isn't. It's just two voices instead of one. I suggested it because a mutual friend told me that Philip was depressed after an operation. I didn't know him all that well, but I thought it might amuse him, prove to be fun. I loved doing it. It was a game.

L.B. & J.R.: If Arthur (Irwin) were here he'd be sitting

in that chair over there and at some point he'd be bound to ask me something like, "Well sir, what do you think about the state of literature in this country?" I want to turn that question on to you.

P.K. PAGE: That's just what he'd ask, isn't it? "Is it going anywhere?" I don't know if I'm up to date on the state of literature in Canada. I think we have a large number of very good poets; too many for their own good because they become invisible in the crowd. There's been a burst of a lot of very good poetry. I'm not as up to date on the state of fiction. Literature will survive. I'm not worried about that. It may be going to fewer and fewer people but it will always survive. It's food.

P.K. 1946

LOIS CRAWLEY

The word "pretty" does nothing to suggest the quality of the girl and it is true that every man in the room was looking at her, or studiously not looking at her, while every woman in the room was looking elsewhere. She sat on a low, square footstool, sat on the edge of it, one foot tucked under her, the other long leg stretched before her. She wore a generous, nubbly skirt, for she was a large girl – quite tall – yet she escaped either being fashionably lean or too bountiful. There was about her a pliant quality. Her movements were slow and direct and this feeling of suppleness was carried out in the long, straight hands, the curveless thumbs. Her presence was immense.

Below the wrist of her long-sleeved black sweater she wore a heavy, dull silver bracelet, very wide and curious. She turned it round and round her wrist with a delicate movement of thumb and forefinger and this slow movement gave to the bracelet a sense of great heaviness, of a great weight being turned by her slender fingers. Two simple hoops of silver hung from her ears, gypsy fashion, swinging against the curve of her cheek. Except for her eyes, you might say her hair was the most striking thing about her. It was very dark – almost black – neither wavy nor curly but tousled in shiny flicks that grew up and down and around her slender neck. As she turned her face more fully into the light, her eyes lost the shadows and shone a lovely, pale green beneath dark brows. Beautiful.

She had been speaking softly but in an animated way to a small group of people and although I could not hear her words, it seemed she had asked a question for she leaned forward, clasping her hands before her, waiting for an answer. A tall, thin man, horn-rimmed, whose reputation for caustic comment was well enough known, leaned back, admired the glowing tip of his cigarette and favored the girl with a patronizing smile and a few thin-lipped words. For a moment she sat rigid, her face turned up to the man, only her eyes darkened, dilated like a cat's. Then her hand strayed to the heavy bracelet, turning it round slowly.

P.K. PAGE

MARILYN RUSSELL ROSE

For P.K. Page, the best poetry is a kind of prophecy and the true poet a visionary of sorts. She speaks of the high calling and special mission of the poet-seer:

> I'm very concerned with the function of the poet, the role of the poet, as I grow older. You have to be worthy of being chosen to be this vehicle. I think that . . . one has to have one's craft at one's finger tips, and one's being in some state of purity . . . burning with some clear enough light that you can become a medium of the highest themes.

This insistence upon the seriousness of poetry and upon the poet's obligation to engage with the "highest themes" has marked Page's work from its beginnings a half century ago, when she, as a young poet with a few published poems to her credit, met Patrick Anderson in Montreal in 1941. It was through Anderson that she was drawn into the small circle of poets (including F.R. Scott, Neufville Shaw, and later A.M. Klein) who would produce the short-lived but influential literary magazine, *Preview* (1942–45). Yet Page's sense of poetry as serious and the poet as having obligations to society at large was well developed even before her connection with *Preview*. Her life while growing up as Patricia Kathleen Page ("Patsy"), the daughter of a Canadian career soldier, had been peripatetic. The family moved after her birth in Swanage, England, in 1916, to Red Deer, Alberta in 1918, and from there to Winnipeg, Calgary, Halifax, and Saint John, New Brunswick (with a year in England along the way). The frequent moves and adjustments to new settings undoubtedly developed in Page an attention to social detail and social difference that would stand her in good stead as a writer. In addition, hers was a family that valued poetry, quoting it liberally at home, and with their encouragement she had begun to write and to publish poems, using her initials, "P.K.," while in her teens.

Indeed her attraction to the arts, and to writing in particular, was clear from the start. After completing high school in Calgary, Page took a position as a salesclerk in the book department of a Saint John bookstore. But she supplemented that job with work more meaningful to her – reading and writing for CBC radio, writing and acting in local theatre, and writing book reviews for local publications. Moreover, as a young woman in the 1930s, she read a great deal of contemporary poetry, finding herself particularly moved by the work of poets like T.S. Eliot, C. Day Lewis, Edith Sitwell, Stephen Spender, and Wilfred Owen – poets of social conscience as well as of a clearly modern sensibility.

And so Page's absorption into the left-leaning *Preview* group, with its insistence upon the modern values of objectivity, intellectuality, compression, and cosmopolitanism –along with a sense of social responsibility – is not surprising, and much of her work during this period reflects these standards. The twelve poems by Page which appear in Ronald Hambleton's *Unit of Five* in 1944, for instance, are marked by empathy for the alienated, the underprivileged, and the oppressed. Poems like "Bed-Sitting Room," "Foreigners," "The Inarticulate," and "Bank-Strike" resonate with the pain of the dispossessed, as does "Snapshot":

> She was dime-dead,
> a silver thing passed as a token from hand to hand
>
> she was quick as money
> and coveted by private fingers,
> fumbled for, clutched, caught and spent
> in a second.

At the same time, even these earliest, most "social realist" of Page's poems are marked by the density of imagery and intensity of language which characterizes so much of her later work. In "Cullen," for example, a series of rich, condensed, almost surrealistic images conveys the boy's horror at the emptiness of the commerce he finds in the city, and its impoverishment of those whom it employs for its own gain: he

> Saw the worm's bald head rise in the clerk's eyes
> and metal lips spew out fantasies;
> saw pink enamel of salesgirls chip and harden
> beneath the outer folds of respectable darkness

as they sold garments they could only touch –
lovely as wind blowing imagined hair,
these webs for the flesh that they would never wear.

Page claims that the *Preview* group "broke my head wide open with the things they knew that I didn't," as the group met weekly and read their works aloud to one another, and certainly her first book of poems, *As Ten, As Twenty* (1946), attests to her development as a poet under their aegis. A number of the poems in this collection continue to focus on those victimized by social forces inimical to the individual. The much – anthologized "The Stenographers" is an example of Page at her most polemical during this period, as it deals with the monotony and sterility of the lives of ordinary clerical workers whose days are a "forced march" from "Monday to Saturday," through a veritable "snow storm of paper." The pitiless voice that "draws their pencil / like a sled across snow" condemns them to climates of "winter and summer – no wind / for the kites of their hearts – no wind for a flight." In the end, the women collapse, driven mad by the callousness of a system that treats people like robots in the name of efficiency:

In the felt of the morning the calico minded,
sufficiently starched, insert papers, hit keys,
efficient and sure as their adding machines;
yet they weep in the vault, they are taut as net
    curtains
stretched upon frames. In their eyes I have seen
the pin men of madness in marathon trim

race round the track of the stadium pupil. (*ATAT,* p.
13)

Other poems in this collection, though, point to
Page's growing interest less in classes or types of
people, or political issues, than in the inner lives of
individuals. In poems like "Only Child" or "The
Landlady," Page describes strangely obsessed individuals whose alienation from humankind is clear and
pathetic. In "Only Child" a boy who wrings the necks
of songbirds, then lays them almost religiously upon
the altar of a "wide maternal lap," is described with
perfect detachment – and our horror in contemplat-
ing a child so cruel is magnified by the distanced,
matter-of-fact tone which the narrator assumes. In
"The Landlady," tenants attempt in vain to hide their
lives from their landlady's scrutiny, but her "camera
eye" is implacable. Feeding like a parasite upon their
lives, she will be satisfied with nothing less than their
total exposure: for she

     . . . like a lover, must know all, all, all.
     Prays she may catch them unprepared at last
     and palm the dreadful riddle of their skulls
     hoping the worst. (*ATAT,* p. 8)

In the most remarkable poem in *As Ten, As Twenty,*
"Stories of Snow," Page moves towards a theme
which will concern her very centrally in her later
work – that of perception, and the way that the
individual mind shapes its own reality, its own world,
as it processes sensation. "Stories of Snow" describes

the exhaustion of those who dwell in the teeming tropics where the "vegetable rain" spawns leaves "large as hands," and where flowers which "protrude their fleshy chins / and call their colours" bar the roads with their brassy "reds and blues." Assaulted, in effect, by rampant sensation, some take refuge in dreams of its opposite – in "stories" of cool, anaesthetizing snow:

> of how, in Holland, from their feather beds
> hunters arise and part the flakes and go
> forth to the frozen lakes in search of swans –
> the snow light falling white along their guns,
> their breath in plumes.
> While tethered in the wind like sleeping gulls
> ice boats wait the raising of their wings
> to skim the electric ice. (ATAT, p. 8)

Raw-nerved "raconteurs," in other words, "unlock / the colour with its complement and go / through to the area behind the eyes / where silent, unrefractive whiteness lies." Page writes here about perception and its transformation into art – the way that consciousness absorbs sensation which is then reconstituted through the imagination. Here "dreams" and "stories" soothe the overstimulated sensibility: the chaos of experience has been converted into cool white space, an area from which stories (that is to say art) can be generated.

All in all, the 1940s represent a period of tremendous growth and productivity for P.K. Page. While maintaining her connection to *Preview* magazine in

Montreal, she published widely in other journals, from *Canadian Forum, Canadian Poetry Magazine, Preview* and *First Statement* to American magazines such as *Poetry (Chicago)*. She also established an important relationship with the encouraging and influential editor of *Contemporary Verse*, Alan Crawley of Victoria, who served as critic and mentor to Page throughout this period. After moving to Victoria with her mother in 1944, Page maintained her connection with another journal, John Sutherland's *Northern Review*, for which she served as West Coast regional editor for a time.

In the meantime, awards and recognition had begun to come her way. In 1944 Page was awarded the Oscar Blumenthal Prize for a group of poems published in *Poetry (Chicago)*, and in 1946 she won the Bertram Warr Award for a selection of poems which appeared in *Contemporary Verse*. In 1944 Macmillan sought to publish her novel, *The Sun and the Moon*, which had been written while she lived in the Maritimes and had been submitted for publication in 1941. Page reluctantly agreed, provided the novel appear under a pseudonym (Judith Cape), for it seemed to her by then that the novel, a kind of fable about a young woman with magical empathetic powers, was "the work of a child" in comparison with the kind of poetry which she was now producing, and she wished to distance herself from it. Indeed, almost forty years would pass before *The Sun and the Moon* – which is more substantial than Page thought then – was published under Page's own name.

Following the Second World War, Page moved to
Ottawa where she worked for the National Film
Board as a researcher and scriptwriter. While there
she met and married William Arthur Irwin, a former
journalist and editor who became chairman of the
NFB in 1950, the year of their marriage. When Arthur
Irwin moved to the diplomatic service in 1953, and
was appointed Canadian high commissioner to Australia, Page's life changed dramatically. The Irwins
spent 1953-56 in Australia, 1956-60 in Brazil, and
1960-64 in Mexico, and the latter two postings in
particular had a dramatic effect on the development
of P.K. Page – as poet and as artist.

While in Australia, Page continued to write, publishing *The Metal and the Flower,* which won the
Governor General's Award for Poetry, in 1954. It is
a remarkably poised collection and one in which Page
can be seen as breaking new ground. Poems like
"Photos of a Salt Mine," "The Permanent Tourists,"
and "Portrait of Marina" take up a familiar theme for
Page, as for many other modern poets – perception,
and the subjectivity inherent in all "seeing."

"Photos of a Salt Mine" speaks most explicitly of
the way that perspective and expectation colour one's
reception of a given experience. Seen through a filter
of innocence, Page tells us, the salt mines are a magical
"Aladdin's cave." Photographs reveal walls that seem
to glitter with rubies and opals, and salt-drifts that
look like the kind of snow children make angels in or
the drifted sheets that lovers imprint with their bodies. But when the perspective changes, as in the last

photo, which is "shot / from an acute high angle" through a filter of "guilt," all innocence is annulled: the men in the pit who "struggle with the bright cold fires of salt / locked in the black inferno of the rock," are seen to inhabit a Dantean universe, a "nether hell" of interminable, backbreaking labour.

Similarly "The Permanent Tourists" reflects Page's interest in pictures and frames and the way they shape the experience they record. Her "terrible," "somnolent," perpetual sightseers wander about, "their empty eyes / longing to be filled with monuments." They stalk statues, memorials, a local hero, "forgotten politicians," and a "stolid queen," all the while refusing to enter into the actual life that surrounds them. Thoroughly apathetic and utterly "incapable of feeling," they then "Lock themselves into snapshots" – in the hopes that these pictures will "conjure in the memory" an excitement, a feeling, which they failed to experience in actual fact. They fabricate experience by way of their photographs, in other words, as a substitute for real experience, and this is a sign of their spiritual impoverishment. At the same time, however, there is a sophisticated irony in the fact that the tourists, as "terrible" as they are, are "beautiful" too: however incomplete their response to what they are seeing, in looking at the plaza they "stamp" it; they call it into life by gazing, even as "placid rivers" revitalize "ruined columns" by reflecting them in their moving waters. That which is "seen" lives and has meaning; that which is not, does not.

"Portrait of Marina" sets pictures against pictures,

viewpoint against viewpoint, and the subject of "seeing" is again the real subject of the poem. First there is Marina's father's picture of "his lost four-master" buoyed up by a Prussian-blue sea, a scene which he has embroidered in "teazled wool" to celebrate what he loves most – not his timid daughter (though she has been conscripted to assist him, and must endlessly thread his needle and bear his oaths) but rather his own lifelong engagement with his worthy opponent, the sea. Then there is the sentimental verbal portrait which his ancestor, the "dimity / young inland housewife," draws of him, the sea captain, her wonderful "great-great-grandpapa": she imagines him "wrapped round in faded paisley shawls / gently embroidering" his picture in heroic triumph over age, arthritis, and cataracts. Marina is absent from this picture too. And finally, placed against both of these, is the narrator's compelling counter-portrait of Marina, the pale spinster daughter, "warped / without a smack of salt," grown "transparent with migraines," brutalized in effect by a father whose tyranny eventually destroys the "trembling edifice" that she has become. She who should have been a "water woman, rich with bells" is in fact so terrified of "Father's Fearful Sea" that she is unable to respond to the coloured stones and pebbles at its shore. Marina's pain is exquisite, and Page's imagery in conveying her agony superb:

> She walked forever antlered with migraines
> her pain forever putting forth new shoots
> until her strange unlovely head became
> a kind of candelabra – delicate –

where all her tears were perilously hung
and caught the light as waves that catch the sun.

So convincing is this portrait of Marina, in fact, that it calls into question those other pictures which the poem has offered, denying their truth. Indeed all portraits are partial, the poem suggests: even the narrator's portrait of Marina in the end must be seen as a product of the filters through which the narrator sees. To see a picture as "true" is to trust the moral capacity, the vision, of the artist who presents it.

"Arras," the most dazzling of the poems in this collection, goes further in raising questions about art and its reception by its audience. A complex poem, which works less through narrative continuity than through a brilliant juxtaposition of images, "Arras" presents a narrator who is examining an arras, an ancient tapestry on which appears a detailed outdoor scene: trees, lawns, and human figures are beautifully arranged, but frozen in time, motionless and silent. Suddenly, mysteriously, the garden is brought to life by the intrusion of "a peacock rattling its rattan tail and screaming." The poet asks what enabled the creature to intrude upon the scene "in furled disguise / to shake its jewels and silk upon that grass," then admits that it was she who unleashed its presence:

> I confess:
> It was my eye.
> Voluptuous it came.
> Its head the ferrule and its lovely tail
> folded so sweetly; it was strangely slim

to fit the retina. And then it shook
and was a peacock – living patina,
eye-bright – maculate! (*MAF,* p. 63-64)

In a sense this is transgression: the imagination of the
observer has "altered" the work of art in contemplat-
ing it; the visionary viewer has recreated the art in
perceiving it. At the same time, however, the vision
of the viewer has injected new life into the artefact,
and this too is a creative, enriching act. The line
between artist and observer, indeed between art and
life, becomes blurred as one realizes that art, like
much of life, exists as much in perception as in fact.

In 1957 Arthur Irwin became Canadian ambassador to Brazil, and Page, accompanying him there,
entered the most extraordinary phase of her life.
"Brazil pelted me with images," she has said. She
found the country incredibly beautiful, wonderfully
baroque in its climate, vegetation and architecture.
The joyful sensuality and spontaneity of Brazilians,
their essential merriness, delighted her. Unable to
speak Portuguese at first, however, she found for a
time "a mute observer, an inarticulate listener, occu-
pying another part of myself." Indeed, finding herself
curiously unable to write poetry at all, she turned
instead to drawing, producing pictures (first in felt
pen, then in media as various as crayon, water colour,
oil, and egg tempura) and eventually exhibiting her
work, in Canada and internationally, under the name
of P.K. Irwin. Various galleries, including the National Gallery of Canada, now own and exhibit her

pictures, and the memoir of Page's years in Brazil, *Brazilian Journal*, which she published in 1987, includes both full-colour and black and white illustrations from that period. Her most recent poetry collection, *The Glass Air* (1991), also includes a number of drawings by "P.K. Irwin," as if to signal the artificiality of segregating Page's artistic identities.

In 1964, Arthur Irwin retired and he and Page settled in Victoria, where they still live. She began to write poetry again, though slowly, producing two new collections, *Cry Ararat! Poems New and Selected* (1967) and *P.K. Page: Poems Selected and New* (1974) over the next decade. Two more books of poetry appeared in the 1980s, *Evening Dance of the Grey Flies* (1981), a collection which includes the visionary short story "Unless the Eye Catch Fire," and *The Glass Air: Selected Poems* (1985). Most recently, a revised edition of *The Glass Air,* a carefully selected, extensive and chronologically arranged selection of Page's best poetry to date, appeared in 1991. In addition, Margaret Atwood has collected Page's short fiction along with her novel, which had been long out of print, producing *The Sun and the Moon and Other Fictions* in 1973.

Clearly Page has enjoyed what George Woodcock has called a remarkable "second poetic wind" since her "retirement" to Victoria, generating a body of work that is admirably rich and varied. A number of her new poems reflect her experience abroad, such as "Bark Drawing" with its evocation of the emu, kangaroo, and goanna of Australia, or "Brazilian

Fazenda" wherein Page recalls her pink house with its "sugar white pillars" and its grills of black lace, and the sight of coffee ripening "like beads on a bush or balls of fire / as merry as Christmas."

Others testify to her continued interest in seeing and framing and naming. In "Cook's Mountains," for example, Cook is said to have created The Glass House Mountains by so naming them. Once the guide announces "the Glass House Mountains up ahead," his listeners can only see them as glass houses, as Cook saw them in his spyglass. The mountains "were there / before he came" but "they were not the same" then: by "naming them" he "made" them something other than they had been.

The most impressive of Page's recent poetry is that which reflects her growing interest in what might be called transcendental or metaphysical experience. This is by no means a real departure for Page, for she has long been attached to the poetry of Rainer Maria Rilke and Federico Garcia Lorca, to that of Archibald Lampman (with its celebration of the transcendent moment), and to that of her *Preview* colleague A.M. Klein, whose work she sees as deeply metaphysical. But her exploration in recent years of Persian poets of the twelfth to fifteenth century and the Sufi philosophy out of which they write, seems to have intensified Page's own metaphysical concerns.

For Page, vision – the ability to see beyond ordinary life, and into a larger reality that lies behind reality as we know it – is a rare gift and one to be nurtured. It involves intuition more than rational processes, and cannot be forced. Thus, while the visionary poet will inevitably yearn towards larger truths, those truths must come to the poet in their own good time, however great the poet's immediate desire for them may be.

Indeed, there is pain in feeling earthbound and longing for release into another, better sphere, as the powerful poem "Leather Jacket" suggests. In it, a peacock – so often an emblem of the psyche or the spirit in Page's work – has been sewn up "in heavy leather," its "pupils sealed," its "light and fluttering heart / heavy as a plum," its "memory / of a fan of feathers" fading, its life become "vegetable." It sees, smells, and hears nothing, confined as it is, and yet it retains a "terrible yearning" for release into a "growing garden" with "sunshine falling / as light as pollen," where its feathers can be unfurled and it will be free. So too do human souls seek to transcend physicality and temporality, and yearn for access to what lies beyond.

"Cry Ararat!" points to that eternal search for the elusive garden just out of one's reach. The title alludes to Noah's sighting of Mount Ararat from his ark, the land that will end his watery exile. For Page the artist-seer is a Noah-like figure who scans the horizon, gifted with eyes and with ears that can sense Ararat – that perfect, promised Edenic garden – as others cannot. Her emphasis is on the grace that permits the artist to see beyond the life that most of us know: her Noah must not strain "to touch . . . nor labour to hear" Ararat but must wait in perfect confidence for the revelation that is, after all, a gift and a boon that cannot be forced. What is clear in the language here, and in the religious framework of the poem, is Page's insistence upon the spiritual nature of the artist's task and the experience of transcendence which metaphysical poetry must attempt to effect.

But perhaps it is "After Rain," an earlier poem (first published in 1956), that best expresses Page's sense of the poet's yearning for special sight and special understanding. In the end, the poet utters a kind of prayer. For her devoted gardener Giovanni, whose joy is all in the ordering of the earthly garden, the poet asks that the birds "choir him" and "let him come to rest" within the beauty of the ripening garden. For herself as poet, however, the supplication is for larger vision, for an ability to see beyond the minutiae of the garden and into the "whole" of things:

> And choir me too to keep my heart a size
> larger than seeing, unseduced by each
> bright glimpse of beauty striking like a bell,
> so that the whole may toll,
> its meaning shine
> clear of the myriad images that still –
> do what I will – encumber its pure line.

Finally, it might be noted of Page's later work that a substantial number of her recent poems are simple, spare, and (given the cool, detached, objective tone of so much of her early work) surprisingly personal. Page acknowledges that this has been a rather strange shift, observing that it is as if she has proceeded "backwards" in comparison to most poets – writing most objectively and with the greatest distance when young, and "now, as I totter into my dotage . . . writing about myself." The personal poems are pleasing and welcome. Lyrics like "Domestic Poem for a Summer Afternoon," in which she and "Arthur" read and doze in the garden on a day so hot they are motionless as decoys, or "For Arthur" which speaks of her devotion to him and ends "I love you, love you," are moving in their intimacy and their delicacy. Similarly, the poems (particularly in *Evening Dance of the Grey Flies*) which speak of aging, illness and death, are genuinely moving. In "Phone Call from Mexico," for example, there is pain, and compassion, in the plain language and the broken rhythms that are underscored by the spacing of the words on the page:

> You are all
> those whom I love
> who age ungainly
> whose
> joints   hearts   psyches
> minds   unhinge
> and whom
> I cannot mend
> or ease . . .

In recent years P.K. Page has been honoured as one of the most accomplished and respected of Canadian writers. She was made an Officer of the Order of Canada in 1977, and received the Banff Prize from the Banff Centre School of Fine Arts in 1989 for her outstanding and continuing contribution to the arts in Canada – both awards of the highest calibre that attest to her achievement and her influence in Canada and beyond.

The awards are well deserved. Page is an outstanding Canadian poet, dazzling in the fecundity of her imagination, in the richness of her language, in the skill with which she assembles intricate images, and in the metaphysical reach of her most complex poems. While her work is frequently difficult and sometimes enigmatic, there is at its heart a substance, a feeling and vision, and an exquisite craftsmanship that richly repays those who give themselves over to it.

ALPHABETICAL

MARNIE PARSONS

P.K. Page's *Alphabetical* (Hawthorne Society / Reference West, 23, $10.00) is a small, elegant offering – a modestly designed and simply made chapbook, it appears in a limited edition of two hundred. There is nothing simple about its text, though. Readers of Page won't be surprised by the intricacies and eloquence of this astonishing alphabet book. Each of its twenty-six poems meditates upon a word beginning with one of the letters of the alphabet. The poems are interwoven; the progression through the alphabet is anticipated by the preceding letter-poem. Thus, the "b" poem plays upon notions of "before," a word that appears in the "a" poem; the "c" poem ponders "care," a word that appears in the "b" poem. The whole ends with a "z" poem dealing with "zero" in which "afterwards," the "a" word, appears.

In fact, Page employs several orders of progression. The sequence is circular, suggesting that language encloses and precedes itself; letters, words, are involved in a self-containing, self-generating system. The sequence follows the standard arbitrary a to z progression of the alphabet. Yet it also reverses such seeming linearity, since it begins with "afterwards" which, Page writes, "(bears) the phantom of *before* within it," and has an aural echo of afterword, the writing which concludes, follows upon, another writing. The sequence ends with zero – a number bearing a striking resemblance to a letter; that contains both beginnings and endings; that is not a number, or signifies no thing; whose shape hints at the movement of the sequence (and the computer graphic bullet that follows each poem), at the circle of infinity, the infinite regress of language to (perhaps?) nothing, or to a particularity, some peculiar ripple in a number system, a language system. An absence made palpable. As Page says:

> How visualize nothingness –
> rare gift from Arabia –
> absence of all magnitude?
>
> And – afterwards?
>
> How anticipate
> afterwards?

The poems are all beautifully turned and any of them could stand independently. But I prefer them in their alphabetic sequence, love how they draw to themselves all sorts of things that seem to stand outside of language. That is the true delight of any alphabet book, the true revelation – not that "b" follows "a," but that the devising mind has associated "a" with apple or Adam or armadillo. An enormous amount can be learned about an individual, a culture, an era from the alphabets it produces, the world its alphabet builds. The alphabets in Puritan primers, for instance, are strikingly different from those written in England or North America today, and express very different understandings of education, knowledge, and individuality. What one gathers from Page's alphabet is a fascinating glimpse into her poetics, a poetic affirmation of a knowing and careful love of words.

Page has written poems about doubt, God, and ignorance, about kissing, love, and need, about paradise (what others call Brazil) and traps. Yet none of these poems is simply *about* these things; rather, they probe how words – "doubt" and the rest – mediate, define, enrich, limit experience.

> *Or* – "a function word
> to indicate an alternative" –
> while giving us choices, narrows our options;
>   is
>   as reductionist as *I* is, O
> eliminate it, take it away, we require
> all the doors and windows open. Remove the roof
> tile by virtual tile, take down the walls.
> Paradise is merely an *or* away. Or is it?

The world is, to a degree, determined by words. Or can be overly determined by them, if we lovers of words forget that language must be lived as well as learned.

These poems move with such grace, with such thoughtfulness and simplicity (something quite other than being simple) that one may well, on first reading, miss their profound intelligence, the wide reach of their embrace. Rereading reveals their beautiful weave. They hold the smallness of a single letter and the fullness of that same letter. The paradox and the promise of language. And they are wise. One can feel the mature wit, the wealth of experience and the true modesty of a fascinating and exacting mind on the move in these words. A gift, this wonderful alphabet enacts one woman's passion for the lived word.

P.K. PAGE: AN OFFERING

CAROL MATTHEWS

Recently I wrote an article about how my husband had made himself a fetish. I spoke of how he had chosen the Congolese name, Mr. Koko. How he'd selected the log, carved it, painted the wide red mouth, glued in the blue chitonshell eyes. Attached driftwood arms and clamshell opercula teeth. Bound the torso with golden-fibred hemp. I sent the piece to my friend P.K. Page who was delighted with the idea of it. Soon afterwards an envelope arrived in the mail, addressed to Mr. Koko, c/o my husband.

Inside was a single sheet of paper on which was a poem, written first in Mr. Koko's own language and followed by a rough translation:

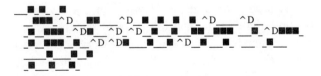

A rough translation:

Offering
> To your seablue eyes I offer human sight.
> To your snag teeth I offer food for your very soul.
> To your little grey arms I offer my embrace.
> Oh, Mr. Koko

Ko, Ko, Ko!

P.K.'s gesture to Mr. Koko, if not representative of her best poetry, is typical of the generous offerings she makes in her work. Sight to eyes that do not see, substance to one's very soul; the invitation to be transformed, the introduction to a new and exotic language: these are all things I find in her writing.

My first encounter with P.K. Page was through her poems, in black and white, the written words arranged perfectly on a page. Through these poems I saw finches feeding like never before, wondrous with their east / west eyes. Through her eyes. My own eyes followed hers in spiralling paths through to the end of the maze. Followed her through backward journeys in the eyes of the mind. Followed the eyes catching fire. For a long time, to me, she was all eye. Observing and observed.

Then I saw her in person, dressed in black and silver, seated on a stage. Swathed in a shawl and, beyond that, in an invisible mantle which set her apart. Lit up by an aura. Luminous. Effervescent. And I saw that her person embodies the spirit of her poems: brilliant, glimmering, filigreed, mercurial.

When I heard her read, I realized that P.K. bodies the spirit of her poems in her voice. After that, her voice was always there. I could no longer see her work without also hearing her voice. In her reading I heard a lake of images, a river of words. The images transforming themselves into sound. And the other way round. I heard the magic way in which she connects vision and voice.

There is always magic in P.K.'s methods. Almost thirty years ago, she wrote an essay entitled "Traveller, Conjuror, Journeyman," in which she discusses connections between writing and painting, between the aural and the visual: "Magic," she notes, "That Great Divide, where everything reverses. Where all the laws change." A good writer or painter understands these laws, she says, and practices conjuration.

And what is it that conjurers do? They do what P.K. Page does. They make things disappear. Re-appear. Transform. In her poems, something as simple as a leaf can make a mountain disappear or come into being. As quick as being sucked through the eye of a macaw. Or a deaf-mute finding a little door in his locked throat. As sudden as a stone dissolving. As enchanting as a drawing of a labyrinth or the detail of *The Dance.* As in "Cry Ararat!":

> A single leaf can block a mountainside;
> All Ararat be conjured by a leaf.

Or "After Donne":

> For the least moving speck
> I neglect God and all his angels
> yet attention's funnel
> a macaw's eye contracts,
> becomes a vortex.
>
> I have been sucked through.

Or "Deaf-Mute in the Pear Tree," in which the deaf-mute, with "A stone in ears and on his tongue" is transformed by the appearance of his wife's face and

> Then air is kisses, kisses
>
> stone dissolves
>
> his locked throat finds a little door
>
> and through it feathered joy
> flies screaming like a jay.

Reading P.K.'s work I find myself led down tricky paths in which disappearance is always a possibility. In "A Backwards Journey" the child knows that

> . . . if no one called
> and nothing broke the delicate jet
> of my attention, that tiny image
> could smash the atom of space and time.

In "The Maze," the speaker follows:

> the spiralling pathway over and over, run
> hoping to pass that place on the sharpening turn
> to grow small, then smaller, smaller still and enter
> the maze's vanishing point, a spark, extinguished.

In *Hologram,* the traveller and conjurer work in tandem, in the writer's journey through the loved poems of her lifetime, and in the alchemy that allows her to mix together two distinct and various voices in order to produce something entirely new. Throughout these poems I have the sense of hearing two voices at the same time, one echoing the other. And I have the impression of being in two places at once – here on earth, grounded in quotidian dailiness, and far away, talking to the angels.

The hologram, in which a previously unseen picture is lit up by an unexpected light, is a particularly appropriate image for P.K.Page's work.

In a hologram, every part contains the information of the whole; any fragment can be lit up to reveal a complete image. This is an ideal tool for a conjurer, and it is surely a conjurer's trick to take a quatrain and open it up like a magician reaching into her sleeve to reveal festoons of flowers or silken scarves. Just so does P.K. work her magic, so that one can never afterward look at the first four lines that inspired these poems without sensing the fuller possibilities lying beneath the surface, ready to burst forth.

In "Request to the Alchemist," Page speaks directly about alchemy and about the transformation she seeks:

> I am a tin whistle
> Blow through me
> Blow through me
> And make my tin
> Gold

She speaks to the alchemist as witches do, just as she

speaks to the wind, in "Big Wind,"or to the tree, in
It is "Like a Cruise Ship":

> Oh tree! I say as I whizz past, bowing. I bow. I whizz
> Powered by some high octane fumeless fuel
> That spring has invented. Oh tree! I say. *Tree. Tree!*

Even after I had been introduced to P.K. Page a
number of times and had long admired her work, it
was years before I dared to approach her directly if I
encountered her on the street or in a bookstore. Not
that she was ever cool or stand-offish, or anything but
gracious. She wasn't exactly friendly, but certainly
always attentive, courteous and charming. Yet I was
intimidated by a quality I saw in her and not others:
a remove, an aura.

Something that set her apart.

It is a real thing, this mantle, this aura, and when
I am with P.K. I can sense her shape-shifting powers,
the invitation to go somewhere else, to become something else. A kind of magic that makes one hesitate.
Reading her poems, though, there is no time to
hesitate. You are immediately drawn in, sucked
through, whizzing and bowing and following the
maze to its vanishing point. The mage, to the place
where she becomes invisible. And you do not return
unchanged.

In all that she does, P.K. Page is a mage, a conjurer,
a transformer. The offering she made, humourously,
to Mr. Koko is what she offers in all seriousness to

her audience: vision, substance, transformation. It is an irresistible invitation. A formidable offering.

GYPSY QUEEN

LINDA ROGERS

"Step on a crack, break your mama's back."

We all say it, in so many languages,
so many mothers bent over with the weight of us,
our belief in rhyming taught to us by them.
"Sticks and stones will break my bones,"
their bones made brittle by leaching,
the constant flow of milk from their breasts,
our first singing teachers.

"What is a poem?" everyone asks. We are
fountains of grief, our bodies depleted,
eroded landscapes by Cézanne, the marble
steps to the Acropolis and the Temple
of the Goddess Athena worn down by men
and women who worship a blinding
sky full of imperfect men, who ride gypsy
wagons pulled by galloping horses.

We are milk hardened into butter.

"Do you like butter?" The first sign of summer
is weeds that come up through pavement cracks
and in fields where animals graze, turning
the chin of every child who asks into gold
mined by Neibelung, little miners searching

underwater for evidence the sun belongs
to anyone with the courage to walk
on the bottom of rivers and lakes and oceans
and say the name of everything she sees:
lost continents, angel fish, drowned men,
especially dandelions, the other golden weed
with comforting leaves and seeds that fall
into cracks that are open and hungry as gypsies
on horses cantering off with praise when she
wishes and blows, four score and more
candles burning in the golden eye of the sun.

This is how she tells time; she counts
the rings on the tree that falls on her
house in a storm and she makes them rhyme.
The tree is free, its roots revealed,
raised up to sing in the morning,
the day they have made and also insects
with jewelled backs that blink in the light.

Some children blink when they tell
stories some adults believe to be lies,
but it is only semaphore, the language
alchemists speak when they turn what they
remember into flecks of gold
in the eye that is hearing what every
child knows to be true and every true poet
can not be allowed to forget.

The alchemist works day and night
in that hidden room behind the eyes,
the very last chakra before the body

turns into air, turning everything golden
into gold, a marmalade cat, a canary,
buttercups, dandelions, daffodils,
primroses, mustard seed, the yellow
brick road to the enchanted city of Oz.

No wonder they're restless,
everything, everyone waiting in line
to put on the white silk scarf that means
she has prayed for them while she spins
and speaks as everything blessed:
sticks, stones, man woman, everything,
everyone you can rub together, glosa,
renga, gypsy herself catches fire.

BIBLIOGRAPHY

Patricia Kathleen Irwin (Judith Cape; P.K.Page; P.K.Irwin).
Writer and artist, born Nov. 23, 1916, Swanage, Dorset, England;
daughter of the late Major General Lionel Frank Page, C.B.,
D.S.O., and Rose Laura (Whitehouse) Page; came to Canada
1919; married W. Arthur Irwin, O.C., LLD, 1950; step-children:
Neal A., Patricia J. Morley, Sheila A. Irving. Lived in England,
Australia, U.S.A., Brazil, Mexico.

EDUCATION

Attended schools in Winnipeg, Calgary and England; studied art
under Frank Schaeffer in Brazil and Charles Seliger in N.Y.;
attended the Art Students' League and Pratt Graphics in N.Y.

CAREER

Sales clerk and radio actress in Saint John, N.B.; filing clerk and
historical researcher in Montreal, P.Q.; co-editor of *Preview*;
regional editor for B.C. of *Northern Review*; script writer for the
National Film Board 1946-50. Conducted workshops at The
Writers' Workshop, Toronto, 1974-77; taught at the University
of Victoria, Victoria, B.C. 1977-78; member of the Advisory Arts
Panel to Canada Council 1976-1979; member of the Editorial
Board of *Malahat Review*.

BIBLIOGRAPHY

Unit of 5. Poems with others. Edited by Ronald Hambleton.
    Ryerson, l944.
The Sun and the Moon. Novel. MacMillan, 1944.
As Ten As Twenty. Poems. Ryerson, 1946.
The Metal and the Flower. Poems. McClelland & Stewart, 1954.
Cry Ararat! Poems New and Selected. McClelland & Stewart,
    1967.

The Sun and the Moon and Other Fictions. Prose. Anansi, 1973.
Poems: Selected and New (1942-1973). Anansi, 1974.
To Say the Least: Canadian Poets from A-Z. Editor. Porcepic, 1979.
Five Poems. The League of Canadian Poets, Toronto, l980.
Evening Dance of the Grey Flies. Poetry and prose. Oxford, 1981.
The Glass Air. Poetry, drawings, essays. Oxford, 1985.
Brazilian Journal. Prose and sketches. Lester & Orpen Dennys, 1987.
A Flask of Sea Water. A fairy tale. Oxford, l989.
The Glass Air: Poems Selected and New, Oxford, l991.
The Travelling Musicians. Kids Can Press, l991.
The Goat that Flew. A sequel to *A Flask of Sea Water.* Beach Holme Press, l993.
Unless the Eye Catch Fire. Short story. Full Spectrum Press, l994.
Hologram: A Book of Glosas. Brick Books, l994.
The Hidden Room: Collected Poems. The Porcupine's Quill, l997.
Alphabetical. A poem. Hawthorne Society Chapbooks, l998.
Rosa dei Vente. Compass Rose. Poems in Italian translated by Francesca Valente. Ravenna: Longo Editore, l998.
P.K. Page / Mimmo Paladino. Toronto: Istituto Italiano di Cultura, l998.

ANTHOLOGIES

Book of Canadian Poetry. Ed. A.J.M. Smith, University of Chicago, 1948.
Other Canadians. Ed. John Sutherland, 1947.
A Book of Canadian Stories. Ed. Desmond Pacey, Ryerson, 1950.
The Blasted Pine. Ed. F.R. Scott and A.J.M. Smith, MacMillan, 1957.
Canadian Poems. Ed. L. Dudek and I. Layton, Contact, 1952.
Twentieth Century Canadian Poetry. Ed. Earle Birney, Ryerson, 1958.
The Penguin Book of Canadian Verse. Ed. Ralph Gustafson, Penguin, 1958.
Canadian Short Stories. Ed. Robert Weaver, Oxford, 1960.
Love Where the Nights are Long. Ed. Irving Layton, McClelland & Stewart, 1962.

The Oxford Book of Canadian Verse. Ed. A.J.M. Smith, Oxford, 1965.

Poetry Mid-Century. Ed. Milton Wilson, McClelland & Stewart, 1964.

Poetry of Our Time. Ed. Louis Dudek, MacMillan, 1965.

Modern Canadian Verse. Ed. A.J.M. Smith, Oxford, 1967.

To Everything There Is a Season. Ed. Roloff Beny, Longmans, 1967.

The Wind Has Wings. Ed. Mary Alice Downie and Barbara Robertson, Oxford, 1968.

How Do I Love Thee. Ed. John Robert Colombo, Hurtig, 1970.

Made in Canada. Ed. Douglas Lockhead and Raymond Souster, Oberon, 1970.

Contemporary Poetry of B.C.. Ed. J. Michael Yates, Sono Nis Press, 1970.

A Little Treasury of Modern Poetry. 3rd Edition. Ed. Oscar Williams, Scribners, 1970.

The Broken Ark. Ed. M. Ondaatje and Tony Urquhart, 1971.

I Am a Sensation. Ed. Goldberg and Wright, McClelland & Stewart, 1971.

40 Women Poets of Canada. Ed. Dorothy Livesay, Ingluvin Press, 1972.

The Oxford Anthology of Canadian Literature. Ed. Robert Weaver and William Toye, 1973. *Skookum Wawa.* Ed. Gary Geddes, Oxford, 1975.

Canadian Poetry: The Modern Era. Ed. John Newlove, McClelland & Stewart, 1977.

Western Windows. Ed. Patricia Ellis, 1977.

The Poets of Canada. Ed. John Robert Colombo, Hurtig, 1978.

15 Canadian Poets Plus 5. Ed. Gary Geddes & Phyllis Bruce, Oxford, 1978.

The Poetry Anthology: 1919-1977. Ed. Daryl Hine and Joseph Parisi, Houghton Mifflin, 1978.

Sound and Sense. Ed. Joseph Perrine, Harcourt Brace Jovanovich, 1982.

The Oxford Book of Canadian Verse. Ed. Margaret Atwood, Oxford, 1982.

Canadian Poetry. Ed. Jack David and Robert Lecker, New Press, 1982.

The World of the Stone Angel. Prentice Hall, 1983.

Illusion. Ed. Geoff Hancock, Aya Press, 1983.

The Norton Anthology of Poetry. 3rd Edition, W.W. Norton and Co.,1983.

An Anthology of Canadian Literature in English. Vol.II, ed. Donna Bennett and Russell Brown, Oxford, l984.

Stories by Canadian Women. Ed. Rosemary Sullivan, Oxford, 1984.

The New Wind Has Wings. Ed. Downey, Robertson, Cleaver, Oxford, l984.

The Norton Anthology of Literature by Women. W.W. Norton and Co., 1985.

The New Press Anthology #2: Best Stories. Ed. Leon Rooke and John Metcalfe, General Publishing, 1985.

The Faber Book of 20th Century Women's Poetry. Ed. Fleur Adcock, Faber, 1987.

Poetry in English. Ed. M.L. Rosenthal, Oxford, 1987.

Elements of Literature. Ed. R. Scholes, Nancy R. Comley, Carl H. Klaus, David Staines, Oxford, l987.

The Heath Introduction to Poetry. Ed. Joseph de Roche, D.C. Heath, 1988.

15 Canadian Poets X 2. Ed. Gary Geddes, Oxford, l988.

The Norton Anthology of Modern Poetry. 2nd Edition. Ed. Richard Ellman and Robert O'Clair, l988.

Literary Experiences. Vol. I. ed. Oster, Iveson, McClay, Prentice Hall, l989.

Poetry by Canadian Women. Ed. Rosemary Sullivan, Oxford, l989.

Singing Down the Bones. Ed. Jeni Couzyn, Livewire, London, 1989.

Modern Poems. 2nd Edition. Ed. Ellman & O'Clair, Norton, 1989.

Tesseracts 3. Ed. Candas Jane Dorsey and Gerry Truscott, Press Porcepic, l990.

The Brick Reader. Ed. Linda Spalding, M. Ondaatje, Coach House, l991.

Bad Trips. Ed. Keith Fraser, Random House, l991.

Worst Journeys. Ed. Keath Fraser, Pan Books, l992.

The HBJ Anthology of Literature, l993.

Writing Away. Ed. Constance Rooke, McClelland & Stewart, 1994.

The Monkey King and Other Stories. Ed. Griffin Ondaatje, Harper Collins, 1995.

The Seashell Anthology of Great Poetry. Ed. Christopher Burns, Park Lane Press, 1995.

20th Century Poetry & Poetics. Fourth Edition, ed. Gary Geddes, Oxford, 1996.

Writing Home. Ed. Constance Rooke, McClelland & Stewart, 1997.

The School Bag. Ed. Seamus Heaney, Ted Hughes, Faber & Faber, 1997.

MAGAZINES

Alphabet; Arc; Ariel; Artscanada; Blackfish; Border Crossings; Brick; Canadian Forum; Canadian Literature; Canadian Poetry Magazine; Contemporary Verse; CVII; The Dalhousie Review; Descant; Ellipse; Encounter; Exile; First Statement; Here and Now; Journal of Canadian Poetry; Matrix; Malahat Review; Northern Review; The Observer; The Ontario Review; Poetry; Poetry Australia; Preview; Prism International; Queen's Quarterly; The Raddle Moon; Reading; Saturday Night; Tamarack Review; Tuatara; Voices; The White Pelican; The West Coast Review; Prairie Schooner.

READINGS

Simon Fraser University; The University of British Columbia; The Banff School of Fine Arts; The University of Alberta; The University of Calgary; The University of Lethbridge; Dalhousie University; Glendon College; The University of Guelph; the University of Victoria; York University; Erindale, Scarborough, University College, Victoria College; Mount Allison; University of New Brunswick; Loyola; Wayne State University, Detroit; University of Windsor; Confederation Centre, P.E.I.; Carleton University; Queen's University; University of Ottawa; Ryerson College; A Space, Toronto; Malaspina College, B.C.; Grant McEwan Com-

munity College, Prince George; The Calgary-Banff Conference;
Harbor Front, Toronto; Fanshawe College, London, Ont.;The
Belfry, Victoria; Arts Alliance, Courtenay, B.C.; The University of
Manitoba; The University of P.E.I.; Mount St. Vincent University,
Halifax; The University of New Brunswick; The Literary Store-
Front, Vancouver; Trent; McGill; Mills Memorial Library, Ham-
ilton; The University of Saskatchewan; The Art Gallery of Greater
Victoria; The Greater Victoria Public Library; Open Space, Vic-
toria; Cariboo College, Kamloops, B.C.; B.C. English Teachers
Association; Canadian Cultural Programmes; Newcome Audito-
rium, Victoria; Poetry Festival, Toronto; The West Vancouver
Community Arts Council; St. Margaret's School, Victoria; St.
Michael's School, Victoria; The Vancouver Public Libraries; The
Adelaide Festival, Australia; The University of Vermont, U.S.A.;
Smith College, U.S.A.; a tour of England; Vancouver Writers
Festival; George Woodcock Symposium; Eden Mills Festival; The
University of Western Ontario; Festival of the Written Arts,
Sechelt; International Harbour Front Festival.

OTHER

The Sun and the Moon, dramatised for C.B.C. radio.

Travellers' Palm, an NFB animated film of the poem of the same
    name.

*Personal Landscape: A Song Cycle.*Music by Bernard Naylor.

Text for *The Travelling Musicians,*music by Murray Adaskin.

Text for *The Travelling Musicians,* music by Ruth Watson Hen-
    derson.

*Arras: A Garden of Cinema,*music by David Scott.

Script and commentary for *Teeth are to Keep,* an animated film
    which won an award at Cannes. Many readings on the CBC.

I-Sphinx, a poem for two voices based on the life of Sibelius, for
    the CBC.

Unless the Eye Catch Fire, dramatised with Joy Coghill and
    performed by her with Robert Cram, flute.

Afterwords for *Emily's Quest* and *The Innocent Traveller,* The
    New Canadian Library, McClelland and Stewart.

Wisdom from Nonsense Land, Press Porcepic.

Still Waters: the Poetry of P.K. Page, Film and video, The National
    Film Board of Canada, l991.
Unless the Eye Catch Fire, performed as a one-woman show by
    Joy Coghill, 1994.
A Children's Hymn, music by Harry Somers, l995.
Subject of a two-part sound feature: *The White Glass,* for CBC
    Ideas, 1996.
A special issue of *The Malahat Review,* l996.
The Margaret Laurence Memorial Lecture, l999.

FORTHCOMING

Unless the Eye Catch Fire. Movie version, directed by Anya
    Tchernakova, with the author playing the main role.
The Invisible Reality, text for an oratorio by Derek Holman.
A Somewhat Irregular Renga, poems with Philip Stratford, for the
    C.B.C.

ART EXHIBITIONS

One woman:Picture Loan Society, Toronto, 1960.
Galeria de Arte Moderna, Mexico, 1962.
Art Gallery of Greater Victoria, B.C., 1965.
Group: Galeria Juan Martin, Mexico, 1961.
Primer Festival Pictorico de Acapulco, Mexico, 1963.
Surrealism in Canada, London Public Library and Art Museum,
    Canada, 1963.
The Mystic Circle, Burnaby Art Gallery, 1973.
Victoria Perspectives, Mido Gallery, Vancouver, 1972.
Dawn, Student Union Gallery, U.B.C., 1975.
The Backroom Gallery, Victoria, l976.
The Burnaby Art Gallery, 1978.
Printmaking in B.C.,1889-1983.
The Art Gallery of Greater Victoria, 1983.
Art in Victoria, 1960-1986.
Art Gallery of Greater Victoria; Brazilian Sketches, 1987.
Maltwood Gallery, University of Victoria.

Graphics reproduced in *Artscanada; Canadian Literature;Malahat Review; Tamarack Review; Planes, Seripress; A Political Art: Essays and Images in Honor of George Woodcock,* edited William H. New, U.B.C. Press.

Art Collections in which represented National Gallery of Canada, Ottawa; Art Gallery of Ontario, Toronto; Vancouver Art Gallery; Art Gallery of Greater Victoria; University of Victoria, etc. and private collections here and abroad.

LISTED IN

Contemporary Poets (St. James); The Writers' Directory; The World Who's Who of Women; International Who's Who in Poetry; Dictionary of International Biography; Literary History of Canada; Creative Canada; The Oxford Companion to Canadian History and Literature; Contemporary Authors, U.S.A.; The World's Who's Who of Authors; Canadian Who's Who.

AWARDS

The Bertram Warr Award for a group of poems awarded by Contemporary Verse, 1940; Oscar Blumenthal Award for a group of poems awarded by *Poetry* (Chicago) 1944; The Governor General's Award in Poetry for *The Metal and the Flower,* 1954; National Magazines Award (Gold) 1985; D. Litt., University of Victoria, 1985; Canadian Authors' Association Literary Award for Poetry, 1985-86; *Brazilian Journal,* short-listed for Governor General's Award for Non-Fiction, and winner of B.C. Book Prizes Hubert Evans Award for non-fiction, 1987; Banff Centre School of Fine Arts National Award, 1989; National Magazines Award (Silver) 1989; Readers' Choice Award, Prairie Schooner for a group of poems, 1993.

HONOURS

Received as a poet by the Academia Brasileira de Letras in Rio de

Janeiro, 1959; Officer of the Order of Canada, 1977; Doctor of Laws (Honoris Causa), University of Calgary, 1989; Doctor of Letters (Honoris Causa), University of Guelph, 1990; Doctor of Laws (Honoris Causa), Simon Fraser University, 1990; Doctor of Letters (Honoris Causa) University of Toronto, June, 1998; Companion of the Order of Canada, 1999.

CRITICAL STUDIES

John Sutherland. "P.K. Page and *Preview*." *Northern Review*, 1942.

John Sutherland. "The Poetry of P.K. Page." *Northern Review*, 1947.

A.J.M. Smith. "Poetry of P.K. Page." *Canadian Literature*, 1971.

Northrop Frye. *The Bush Garden*. Toronto: Anansi, 1971.

S. Namjoshi. "Double Landscape." *Canadian Literature*, 1976.

Michel Preston. "The Poetry of P.K. Page: A Check List." *West Coast Review*, 1977.

Constance Rooke. "P.K. Page: The Chameleon and the Centre." *Malahat Review*, Jan. 1978.

Rosemary Sullivan. "A Size Larger than Seeing: The Poetry of P.K. Page." *Canadian Literature*, 1978.

Jean Mallinson. "Retrospect and Prospect." *West Coast Review*, 1979.

George Woodcock. "P.K. Page." *The Oxford Companion to Canadian Literature*. Toronto: Oxford University Press, 1983.

John Orange. *P.K. Page: An Annotated Bibliography*.

The Annotated Bibliography of Canada's Major Authors, Vol. Six, Ed. Robert Lecker and Jack David, Toronto: ECW Press, 1985.

Marjorie Body. "Traveller, Conjuror, Journeyman. P.K. Page: A Profile." *Cross Canada Writers' Quarterly*, 1987.

George Woodcock. "P.K. Page." *U.S.A. Dictionary of Literary Biography*. Bruccoli Clark Layman, Inc., Columbia, S.A., 1988.

John Orange. *P.K. Page and Her Works*. Toronto: ECW Press, 1990.

Forthcoming: A literary biography by Sandra Djwa.

CONTRIBUTORS

Margaret Atwood is a poet and novelist.

Brian Bartlett is a Maritime teacher, poet and essayist.

Lucy Bashford is assistant editor of the *Malahat Review.*

Barbara Colebrook Peace published *Kyrie* with Sono Nis in 2001.

Lois Crawley as the daughter of Page's good friend Alan Crawley gives us the child's eye view of the young poet.

Travis Lane is a Maritime poet and essayist. Her new collection of poetry, *Keeping Afloat,* was published by Guernica in 2001.

Carol Matthews teaches at Malaspina College.

Susan Musgrave is a poet, novelist and reviewer who lives in Sidney, B.C..

Kelly Parsons is a Victoria poet who has published with Reference West and Sono Nis Press.

Marnie Parsons lives in St. John's, Newfoundland, where she edits and reviews poetry, and works at a children's book store.

Harold Rhenisch is a poet, novelist and creator of the youth website for the League of Canadian Poets.

Linda Rogers writes poetry and fiction for adults and children. Her essay from *The Broad Canvas: Portraits of women,* appears courtesy of Sono Nis Press.

Marilyn Russell Rose is chair of the English department at Brock University. She has published a number of articles on Canadian writers.

Jay Ruzesky is a teacher at Malaspina College, author of several books of poetry and editor of Outlaw Editions.

Patricia Young, the author of many books of poetry, the most recent being, *Ruin and Beauty,* is a former student and present friend of P.K. Page.

AGMV Marquis

MEMBER OF SCABRINI MEDIA

Quebec, Canada
2001